INTEGRITY MATTERS:
BE YOUR WORD

BUILDING A SUSTAINABLE COMPLIANCE &
INTEGRITY PROGRAM THAT WORKS

By Dr. Robyn S. Joppy

INTEGRITY MATTERS: BE YOUR WORD
Building a Sustainable Compliance & Integrity Program That Works
Published in the United States by WMS Press, Boston MA

For any ordering information or special discounts for bulk purchases, please contact
Info@oneaccordconsultingfirm.com

INTEGRITY MATTERS: BE YOUR WORD
Building a Sustainable Compliance & Integrity Program That Works

By WMS Press
ISBN-13: 978-1-732342569

2nd Edition, May 1st, 2019
Printed in the United States of America

DEDICATION

I dedicate this book foremost to my mother, the late Amanda E. Hodge-Joppy, who instilled in me the love of God, family, life, friends, travel, and learning. My mother encouraged me not only to dream, but to dream big and pursue my dreams with all fervor. Second, to my father Robert L. Joppy and my sisters Shelley D. Joppy and Toyia L. Joppy-Talley, my number one fans: Thank you for all your love, support, and encouragement every time I dare to dream. Third, to my late uncle, Pastor Albert L. Walker who lived a life of integrity and was the epitome of love. He never failed to remind me "The best is yet to come baby." Finally, to all my extended family, church family, and dearest friends, you mean the world to me.

TABLE OF CONTENTS

ACKNOWLEDGMENTS

I have been extremely blessed and fortunate to have the support and prayers of so many extraordinary people throughout my life. I would like to thank my dedicated family and friends who I call my loves and heart beats and who unselfishly work around their schedules to ensure that I have what I need. Thank you, Evangelist Donna M. Humphries, Pastor Marcus Rivers, Ali and Markita D. Collins, James and Cynthia Rowe, T. Latrice Glanton, Robyne Heath-Carrasquillo, Joy Washington, and Derrick Hodge. Additionally, I am grateful for my peers and colleagues who challenge me to take risks and excel; thank you Global Success Society (GSS), Dr. Kristen Betts, Dr. Robert Scott, Dr. Nicole Huff, Dr. Deborah Johnson, and Dr. Antonio Galan.

FOREWORD

Full disclosure. I have known Dr. Robyn S. Joppy for well over 25 years. My first introduction to Robyn occurred on the campus of Syracuse University when she was a speaker at a rush event for what would soon become my beloved sorority, Alpha Kappa Alpha Sorority, Incorporated. Even back then as an undergraduate Robyn's poise and polish were well-formed but more importantly, she had an earnest and straightforward presence that was magnetic. I can still remember Robyn's speech as she told a room full of eager young women something along the lines of," *if you are here for the pretty colors and the prestige you are in the wrong place. We are focused on service and helping others. If you are not prepared to serve others this is not the organization for you.*" And she said it with that disarming and welcoming smile that was and is sincere and heart-warming. Robyn was the kind of person who was going to tell it to you straight. But with love. Whoa! What a first impression.

As we graduated and our careers took separate paths, I recall a casual conversation we had years later when she said, "you know Valerie you should go into compliance, you would be perfect for that kind of work". At that time in the early 2000's I had never heard of compliance, but I had long since learned that Robyn does not give advice without careful consideration. I decided to look into the field but kind of stored it in my mental back pocket for future reference. And then Enron happened.

I was working at KPMG in the marketing department having abandoned my legal career after failing to find a path that felt right to me. From my vantage point at the firm I had a front row seat to the dire consequences of Enron's self-imposed obliteration. As an employee of a major accounting firm I also witnessed Arthur Anderson's implosion. The E&Y, PWC and Deloitte feeding frenzy for Andersen's top-tier clients is a rarely discussed episode in the dark aftermath of Enron's devastating impact on employees, shareholders and the markets. Life savings, stellar and promising careers, confidence in America's financial system - all lost. Throughout the ordeal a refrain began to emerge: Enron was the story of a failure of something called "compliance".

As I recalled Robyn's advice, I began to research the field. For me a career in compliance represented an opportunity to do good within a corporate context. Because of Enron I began to see the possibility of a legal career that was focused on helping corporations to do the right thing by its employees, its shareholders and the public. After Enron I began to embark on a career in compliance and never looked back.

As I pursued the path that Robyn instinctively knew was right for me, I watched Robyn's career grow from a local compliance practitioner in Pennsylvania, to a nationally recognized industry leading professional, to her now global reputation as an expert in the field. In *Integrity Matters. Be Your Word! Building a Sustainable Compliance & Integrity Program That Works*, Dr. Joppy synthesizes her expertise into a straightforward guide that tells you everything you need to know to excel as a compliance professional.

At the heart of her message is a word of caution similar to the words she shared with a group of wide-eyed candidates so long ago. Compliance is all about service. If you are considering compliance for purely economic reasons as a means to a potentially lucrative career, then you are in the wrong place. Serving others takes integrity. Compliance is not a career for the faint of heart.

Valerie Capers Workman, Esq., Associate General Counsel, Compliance – Tesla, Inc

1

INTRODUCTION

In the first decade of the 21st century, companies like Enron, WorldCom, HealthSouth, and Arthur Anderson led conversations regarding corporate scandals and business ethics (Mensch, 2006). According to Arnold, Arnold, and Arnold (2010), the epic failure of these former "corporate giants" can be imputed to poor organizational culture, poor leadership, and the misconduct of a few bad employees. While culture molds workplace values and standards, the ramifications of a bad or poor corporate culture can be negative and catastrophic. Corporate or organizational malfeasance is attributed to a company's culture, so the federal government recommended the development of a corporate Compliance program as a viable solution.

A compliance program, also known as an integrity or ethics program, is an organization's commitment to adhere to all laws, regulations, internal policies and procedures that govern its business. Johnson (2004) defines **a Compliance program as a program an organization has to help guide them under established laws, regulations, specifications, and policies**. Assessing organizational culture is intended to indicate the significance of ethical conduct and values incorporated into legislative and regulatory reforms. The United States Sentencing Commission (USSC) suggests the primary indicator of success in any Compliance program is the culture of the organization (Johnson, 2004). A compliance program's framework includes monitoring and promoting an organization's established values and depends on hiring employees whose values align with the culture. It encourages employee education and training. The premise behind this strategy is to cultivate a culture based on what is real and what is desired so there will be no deviation (Arnold et al., 2010). Education, and training, are critical to compliance in any industry. Mensch 2006) states ethical training, along with other relevant forms, is imperative for all employees at every level throughout an organization.

When the economic forecast is negative, organizations seek guidance from regulations and legislation to ameliorate their culture and control the risks of organizational failure (Arnold et al., 2010). Establishing a Compliance program within these organizations is perceived as an expense the organization can't afford and that puts them at risk for noncompliance with federal and state regulations. Although the federal government requires organizations receiving Medicare and Medicaid funding to have a Compliance program and a compliance officer, there are non-profit organizations that are noncompliant.

Greenlee and Bukovinsky (1997) indicate there are benefits to having a Compliance program despite the expense; it is one way to detect and prevent violations of laws, regulations, and internal policies and procedures. When a company complies with all laws and regulatory requirements that govern its business, the potential for financial penalties, reputational harm, and disbarment from federal programs are minimized and/or eliminated. The general concept of compliance is the relationship formed by senior leadership's control of the organization's business activities and by the orientation of employees to the leadership's authority (Mackessy, 2010).

There are 1.41 million non-profit organizations in the United States that contribute approximately $905.9 billion to the economy (McKeever, 2015). According to the National Center for Charitable Statistics (2012), tax-exempt organizations include public charities, private foundations, and organizations (e.g., chambers of commerce, civic leagues, fraternal organizations, religious, neighborhood associations, etc.). While non-profit human services organizations are recognized for their charitable giving and volunteering, these organizations must be in compliance and must be able to validate their program's success and impact on the culture. Due to corporate scandals, non-profits remain under mounting pressure to substantiate effectiveness by documenting performance outcome measures as the political, funding community, and public demand accountability and transparency (Carman, 2009).

Compliance education and training, a significant part of a compliance program, are the most effective ways an organization can affect employee conduct and influence the corporate culture. Unfortunately, it is difficult for organizations to pinpoint metrics to measure the impact training, or the evaluation of non-profit performance, e.g. organizational capacity, human resource capacity, technical capacity, and administrative capacity has on the ethical culture (Houlihan, 2015). Lee (2014) distributed an online survey to 828 non-profit human services organizations to examine the variances in the measurement of their performance. Lee's research demonstrated inconsistencies in what is relevant such as outcomes versus output, for measurement.

Regulatory compliance is an organization's adherence to laws, regulations, guidelines, and specifications relevant to its business. Additionally, regulatory compliance is a critical part of a Compliance program and is often used interchangeably with the concept. Violations of regulatory compliance regulations often result in legal consequences, including fines and penalties. Like regulatory compliance, a compliance program, also known as integrity or ethics program, is an organization's commitment to adhere to all laws, regulations, internal policies and procedures that govern its business. Johnson (2004) defined a Compliance program as a program an organization has to help guide them under established laws, regulations, specifications, and policies. The general concept of compliance is the relationship formed by senior leadership's control of the organization's business activities and by the orientation of employees to the leadership's authority (MacKessy, 2010). When a company complies with all laws and regulatory requirements that govern its business, risk(s) are minimized and/or eliminated.

HISTORICAL PERSPECTIVE OF REGULATORY COMPLIANCE PROGRAMS

MacKessy (2010) states modern compliance programs have been around since the 20th century when public safety agencies emerged. Beginning in the 1970s, these programs saw a shift from centralized government oversight to a public model of oversight due to the growing number of organized labor unions. As time passed, each decade was wrought with a corporate scandal causing the government to enact laws to address infractions. The Foreign Corrupt Practices Act (FCPA) was signed into law in 1977 because of an investigation that disclosed hundreds of United States (US) companies bribed foreign officials to secure contracts and bidding privileges. The procurement scandal was an event in the 1980s while Hedge funds and the banking industry's misconduct were at the forefront of the 1990s. In response to the increase in corporate scandals and inconsistency in criminal sentencing, the US Sentencing Commission established federal sentencing guidelines in 1991 that lists seven elements of an effective Compliance program (United States Sentencing Commission, 2014). Beginning in 2001, the criminal trials of accounting firm Arthur Andersen, Enron, WorldCom, and others caused organizations to create or update their compliance program. The literature revealed, in a survey conducted in 2005 by the non-profit Open Compliance and Ethics Group, that 54% of existing compliance and integrity programs were established in 2000-2005 (Aguilar, 2006). In 2014, a report published by the Health Care Compliance Association indicated compliance and integrity programs were continuing to increase in budget and staffing.

UNDERSTANDING THE NEED FOR A COMPLIANCE OFFICER AND A COMPLIANCE PROGRAM

Today's compliance officer must be a strategic business partner and understand the importance of aligning compliance investments with corporate strategies and priorities (Quinlan, 2015). As regulatory bodies increase demands on organizations for board governance and oversight, risk management, and compliance, the compliance officer's role increasingly rises in importance to the level of a Chief Executive Officer (DePippo, 2011).

The research suggests the deluge of corporate scandals, growing mandates, and laws are reasons compliance program s are necessary. According to Mensch (2006), several large and profitable companies "failed as the result of illegal accounting practices and the public scandals that followed" (p. 23). Former corporate giants such as MCI, Enron, HealthSouth, WorldCom, and Tyco are a few organizations that gained notoriety for their unethical business practices. Some corporate executives served prison sentences while the economic viability of the companies was devastated, and stakeholders' assets depleted (Mensch, 2006).

In November 2001, Enron, which was America's seventh largest company, collapsed due to illegal and unethical accounting practices. Although the company had a code of conduct, corporate executives engaged in fraudulent activities. Some activities included: "Unduly aggressive earnings targets and management bonus compensation based on those targets, excessive interest by management in maintaining stock price or earnings trend through the use of unusually aggressive accounting practices, inability to generate sufficient cash flow from operations while reporting earnings and earnings growth, and significant related party transactions" (Thomas, 2002, para. 29).

Following the Enron debacle, the world would learn about Tyco less than one year later. According to Symonds (2002), Tyco's former CEO L. Dennis Kozlowski "reigned supreme." In June 2002, the Securities and Exchange Commission (SEC) accused Kozlowski of stealing hundreds of millions of dollars in unauthorized loans which he used for a lavish personal lifestyle as well as his co-conspirators at Tyco, family, and friends. The organization was accused of having major conflicts of interest, e.g. independent directors had direct financial relationships with the company (Symonds, 2002). This case caused many to wonder how and why Mr. Kozlowski got away with fraud, why the board of directors, PricewaterhouseCoopers, Tyco's external auditor, and the SEC did not detect fraud.

Reports demonstrated companies like Enron and Tyco got away with unethical behavior for so long because no one person or department had responsibility for monitoring and oversight. With Tyco, Kozlowski controlled all communication regarding internal audits that should have been reported to the board of directors by internal auditors (Symonds, 2002). To address the issues, Sarbanes-Oxley (SOX) was signed into law on July 30, 2002. SOX was the government's remedy for accounting reform; it mandated that every organization, regardless of size, had to comply with guidelines established by the SEC. SOX required both leadership and employees receive ethics and compliance plan awareness training (Mensch, 2006). Quinlan (2015) indicated organizations should have one person responsible for providing oversight of the compliance program, who can interpret laws/regulations, and lead discussion on corporate policies and procedures.

IMPACT OF REGULATORY COMPLIANCE PROGRAM ON ETHICAL CULTURE

The literature implicates that compliance be part of all government-required compliance program s. To be in compliance, Trevino and Nelson (2007) recommend organizations include other government mandates besides the United States Federal Sentencing Guidelines (USFSG) seven elements of an effective Compliance program as part of their compliance program; those mandates stipulate a code of conduct, a system of penalties for breaches, and whistleblowing protection. Penalties under the USFSG for unethical misconduct or illegal activity is mitigated by an organization's adherence to its own Compliance program (Arnold et al., 2010). There is skepticism about organizations solely relying on a Compliance program to meet regulatory requirements and the impact it has on the ethical culture due to costs and expense when monitoring legal compliance. Paine (2003) states relying on a Compliance program alone is a short-term strategy that may address crisis management issues but will not affect long-term cultural change. According to Weaver, Trevino, and Cochran (1999), compliance has minimal effect on corporate culture unless more than a basic Compliance program is in effect.

Code of conduct. Jam, Rehman, Kamran, and Yameen (2012) states a code of conduct is ethical values and guidelines that are "a subset of organizational culture, representing a multidimensional interplay among various 'formal' and 'informal' systems of behavioral control" (p. 164). The code of conduct included in the Compliance program is an organization's guide that informs employees and other constituents about the rules and expectations leadership expects all to follow. A reason to place importance on ethical value is that all employees must endeavor to be ethical in their actions and behavior (Valentine & Johnson, 2005). The literature supports a code of conduct strongly emphasizing ethical values is influential in enhancing and changing social responsibility among the leadership and employees (Jam, Rehman, Kamran, & Yameen, 2012). When an organization has no code of conduct, the leadership should agree on identifying the values and morals relevant to the conduct of its employees, board members, and constituents.

EDUCATION AND TRAINING

Compliance education and training are essential to every employee of an organization, therefore, all employees should be properly trained and held to the same standards. Compliance education and training programs represent an organizations' commitment to investing in building a strong ethical culture that strives to adhere to legal and regulatory requirements (Houlihan, 2015). It makes sense for compliance program s to require senior leadership to attend compliance education and training with their subordinates and other employees of the organization for every employee to mutually understand the organization's expectations and see leadership's commitment to the Compliance program (Mensch, 2006). The expectation is that leadership sets the tone in the organization and subordinates look to them for guidance. When employees witness leadership "doing the right thing," exemplifying integrity, and holding everyone to the same standards, employees will generally follow suit.

As the government continues to advance its initiatives to stop fraud, waste and, abuse in federally and state-funded programs, along with the public's demand for accountability and responsibility, compliance professionals are challenged to meet arduous training objectives that address behavioral change and support legal ramifications. Additional research reveals that ethics and compliance training represent a significant portion of the Compliance program budget and is probably the largest item of the compliance tasks (Bennett & Freeden, n.d.). Even so, some non-profit organizations are not investing in education and training as required by regulation. According to Mensch (2006), a major concern when employees attend education and training programs is whether they apply what was learned when they return to their job. It is difficult to identify metrics that quantify the impact training has on an organization (Houlihan, 2015).

NEW EMPLOYEE ORIENTATION

New employee orientation (NEO) is a positive way to educate new employees about an organization's vision, mission, values, and leadership; it assures that all employees begin employment with the exact information on relevant matters (Schmidt & Akdere, 2007). According to Schmidt and Akdere (2007), determining the effectiveness of NEO including if new employees learn during the training and whether the learning is transferred to their job is complicated to answer because of the amount of research on the topic. Learning about the organization's vision, code of conduct, and leadership should not stop after orientation training. A research study showed a major difference in the understanding of the aforementioned subjects before and after NEO (Schmidt & Akdere, 2007).

Orienting new employees to an organization can also be a method for socialization (Hellman, 2000). Mathis and Jackson (2003) state "initial orientation is known to enhance the socialization process, employees' perceptions of the work environment, and the performance of work" (p. 276). A discussion of ethics and the code of conduct during NEO is inclined to provide an understanding of ethics communication within the organization and is perceived as being more important than individual awareness (Valentine & Johnson, 2005). This approach leads people to believe an overview of ethics and the code of conduct during NEO can influence employees to embrace ethical beliefs and have career longevity (Mathis & Jackson, 2003).

EMPLOYEE PERSPECTIVE OF LEADERSHIP

The actions, words, and decisions made by leadership set the tone of an organization. Leadership should assure their organization's compliance plan adopt a top-down approach because lower-level employees and others are likely to take compliance seriously if senior leadership embraces it (Mensch, 2006). Research shows employees look to leadership during times of crisis and uncertainty, so leadership should help create a value-based compliance program, consider how they allocate resources, how they provide modeling and coaching opportunities, and which behaviors they reward and punish (National Business Ethics Survey, 20005).

In 1999, Weaver, Trevino, and Cochran concluded "executives who are committed to ethics are likely to encourage a values-oriented approach to ethics management" (p. 45). Managers cast their viewpoint or attitudes on other people and those leaders committed to ethics can project their stances onto their employees. Therefore, when a call to action for employees to "do the right thing," arises, these leaders expect both their colleagues and employees to respond positively; they desire to build a culture where everyone is committed to shared ethical values (Weaver, Trevino, & Cochran, 1999). For example, the Levi Strauss & Company's former CEO Haas' position regarding their ethical culture states "We all want a Company that our people are proud of and committed to...We want our people to feel respected, treated fairly, listened to and involved" (Weaver, et al., 1999, p. 45).

According to Weaver et al. (1999), values and compliance orientation, also known as a compliance plan, are interconnected; leaders committed to ethics encourage their organizations to develop and implement a compliance plan. Leaders who are committed to an ethical culture are attuned to employees' expectations regarding equity and justice; all employees should be held to the same standards, e.g. rewards and discipline.

Sabir, Iqbal, Rehman, and Yameen (2012) explained an organization's success is based on employee performance. Leaders and organizational members/employees must be able to work independently and collectively to assist the organization in attaining corporate goals and objectives. Additionally, the organization through its leadership will establish expectations. Sabir et al. (2012) suggested when situations or crisis occur, "employees try to fill these expectations, but in some cases, they are dependent on their bosses or management for proper guideline" (p. 165).

EMPLOYEE ATTENDANCE AND LONGEVITY

The cost of employee turnover in organizations can be attributed to three factors: recruitment, training, and lost productivity (Trevino & Nelson, 2007). According to Hellman (2000), companies spend a notable amount of money on orientation programs and believe it is appropriate to use NEO to create a sense of loyalty and commitment to the organization. Hellman (2000) indicated corporate loyalty has both advantages and disadvantages, however; research shows that loyalty to an organization results in low absenteeism and low turnover.

The impact a Compliance program has on an organization's ethical culture is open for debate. The research indicates there is the uncertainty of the impact when other factors are not considered along with the compliance program. Additionally, the research illustrated the relevance of having a set of core standards, the code of conduct, which establishes the organization's expectations. A Compliance program that promotes the need for education and training, particularly during NEO, builds a strong ethical culture. Having well-informed employees helps to lower and/or eliminate risk(s) (Trevino & Nelson, 2007).

REGULATORY NON-COMPLIANCE

The second section of this literature review focuses on regulatory non-compliance. An overview of organizations sanctioned for noncompliance and the consequences for non-profit organizations' noncompliance is discussed.

RISKS AND NON-COMPLIANCE

There are organizations, like the healthcare industry, that operate in a highly-regulated environment comprised with a myriad of identifiable risk areas (Trevino & Nelson, 2007). For example, non-profit human services organizations serving people who receive Medicaid Home and Community-Based Services (HCBS), including individuals with disabilities, are subject to the Home and Community-Based Services Rule. The Medicaid program covers long-term care services in various settings and programs such as HCBS; individuals receiving these services can be supported in their personal residence or in the community instead of being institutionalized.

States administering HCBS must assure the health and safety of people, specifically that providers/organizations and facilities meet state standards, licensure, and certification requirements. Federal guidelines require that documentation exists to validate the eligibility of the HCBS recipient, services are provided under an individual's Individual Service Plan (ISP), and that services were actually provided. According to the Centers for Medicare and Medicaid Services (CMS) (2015), improper HCBS payments can occur when Medicaid funds are incorrectly paid, e.g. wrong amount, not supported by documentation or policy, or used for services not detailed in an individual's ISP. CMS indicated "there are some promising practices that can be integrated into daily practice to correct a majority of the errors found" (CMS, 2015). An effective Compliance program can assist an organization to rectify those risks and meet regulatory requirements. Besides the recoupment of improper payments, the government can impose various sanctions on businesses that participate in fraudulent activity and the ability to demonstrate compliance with regulatory requirements is essential (Bower, 2011).

ORGANIZATIONS SANCTIONED FOR NONCOMPLIANCE

The fall of companies such as Enron, WorldCom, Adelphi, Tyco, HealthSouth, and MCI had people around the world talking about business ethics (Mensch, 2006). These organizations have similar reasons for their demise that can be attributed to leadership misconduct. The literature shows the reasons some organizations failed include: leadership misrepresenting earnings reports, embezzling funds, filing false claims, and using illegal methods to conceal the true financial status of the company (Zimmerman, 2006).

When WorldCom failed in 2002, the organization went into bankruptcy. Then the former CEO, Bernie Ebbers, was convicted and sentenced to 25 years in prison for devising an $11 billion accounting fraud scheme (di Stefano, 2005). Prior to its demise, WorldCom aggressively pursued opportunities for acquisitions. As the telecommunication industry faced an industry-wide downturn, Ebbers falsified financial statements to demonstrate increases in income and revenue. Additionally, Ebbers falsified documentation to portray continual growth in his net worth to ultimately protect his personal financial situation (di Stefano, 2005).

In the early 2000s, HealthSouth, which was a corporate network of rehabilitation hospitals, was on track for great success; the organization had centers in all 50 states, employed over 40,000 employees, a fleet of corporate jets, and a spot on the Fortune 500 list (Thomas, 2011). In March 2003, HealthSouth's former leadership, Aaron Beam, CFO until 1997, Wes Smith, CFO, and Richard Scrushy, chairman and CEO, were accused of fraud. Wes Smith replaced Beam as CFO in 2001. According to Thomas (2011),

"Beam alleged he allowed Scrushy to bully him and other Health-South executives into manipulating financial reports to reflect the numbers Scrushy promised investors" (para. 5). Ultimately, Beam served three months in prison, Smith served fourteen months in federal prison, and Scrushy served seven years on charges unrelated to this case.

The common thread among HealthSouth, WorldCom, and the other one-time corporate giants, was the lack of board governance, lack of effective internal audits and protocols, and no single person responsible for compliance monitoring and oversight. According to Zimmerman (2006), the depth of corporate scandals run deep within organizations; scandals affect employees and shareholders in addition to the stock market and national economy.

CONSEQUENCES FOR NON-PROFIT ORGANIZATIONS' NONCOMPLIANCE

The non-profit sector is susceptible to fraud and the ramifications due to losses is far-reaching. Fraud can negatively affect a non-profit organization's reputation, future funding, ability to focus on its mission, and possibly loss of its 501(c)(3) status (Archambeault, Webber, & Greenlee, 2015). The literature confirmed a reason for fraud in non-profit organizations is a lack of internal controls. Developing and implementing a plan, that includes board oversight, to improve internal controls is a way to minimize and/or eliminate fraudulent activity. However, a cost is associated with implementing a new system. Although non-profit organizations must adhere to the whistleblower protection and record retention provisions under SOX, they are not mandated to follow SOX corporate governance requirements; many have voluntarily adopted SOX best practices regarding internal controls. Organizations which add internal financial audits and controls, administrative controls including employee background checks, develop a confidential fraud reporting protocol, and educate employees about policies and procedures related to fraud can experience benefits by being proactive (Archambeault, et al., 2015). These initiatives resemble a compliance program.

The United States Federal Sentencing Guidelines established the criteria an organization is expected to follow when building its compliance program. Since the amendment of the guidelines in 1991, there have been significant changes to the purpose of an effective compliance program. According to Johnson (2004), the primary purpose shifted from primarily detecting and preventing criminal conduct to including a culture that promotes ethics. For those organizations that implement a Compliance program based on regulatory standards, the FSGO allows for leniency when faced with potential penalties (Debold, 2010). The penalties are severe and can include hefty fines, probation, community service, restitution, and loss of 501(c)(3) status (Greenlee & Bukovinsky, 1997).

Greenlee, Fischer, Gordon, and Keating (2007) suggest it is easier to steal from non-profit organizations than from for-profits because of this perception: they are trustworthy, have challenges in validating revenue streams, weaker internal controls, and reliance on volunteer board members increases vulnerability. Some organizations operate in a highly regulated environment and an effective Compliance program can assist these organizations to meet regulatory requirements.

LITERARY REVIEW REFERENCES

Archambeault, D. S., Webber, S., & Greenlee, J. (2015). Fraud and corruption in U.S. nonprofit entities: A summary of press reports 2008-2011. *Nonprofit and Voluntary Sector Quarterly, 44*(6), 1194-1224. doi:10.1177/0899764014555987

Arnold, D. H., Arnold, K., & Arnold, V. J. (2010). Managing ethical risks and crises: Beyond legal compliance. *Beijing Law Review, 1*(1), 1-6. Retrieved from http://www.proquest.com/

Bader, G. (2007). *Developing a measurement system for the pharmaceutical compliance process using the balanced scorecard.* (Doctoral dissertation). Retrieved from ProQuest Dissertations and Theses. (Order No. 1449537)

Bennett, M. & Fredeen, I. (n.d.). *Eight ethics & compliance training myths debunked.* Retrieved from http://www.corporate-complianceinsights.com/wp-content/uploads/2014/10/navex-onlinetrainingebook-final.pdf/

Bower, J. (2011). How effective is your compliance training? *Journal of Health Care Compliance, 13*(6), 37-40. Retrieved from http://www.proquest.com/

Carman, J. G. (2009). Nonprofits, funders, and evaluation: Accountability in action. *The American Review of Public Administration, 39*(4), 374-390. doi:10.1177/0275074008320190

Centers for Medicare and Medicaid Services. (2015, October). *Home and Community-Based Services. Self-directed home and community-based services*. Retrieved from https://www.cms.gov/Medicare-Medicaid-Coordination/Fraud-Prevention/Medicaid-Integrity-Education/Downloads/hcbs-tk1-gen-overview

Debold, N. C. (2010). US sentencing commission amends requirements for effective compliance program. *Insights: The Corporate & Securities Law Advisor, 24*(6), 10+. Retrieved from http://www.go.galegroup.com/

DePippo, C. (2011). The evolving role of the compliance officer. *Corporate Compliance Insights*. Retrieved from http://www.corporatecomplianceinsights.com/evolving-role-of-chief-compliance-officer/

Dillon, B. (2012). Organizational leadership and the balanced scorecard: Lessons to be learned from marketing activities in a nonprofit setting. *International Journal of Business and Social Science, 3*(15). Retrieved from http://www.proquest.com

di Stefano, T. F. (2005, August 19). WorldCom's failure: Why did it happen? Retrieved from http://www.ecommercetimes.com/story

Ethics Resource Center. (2005). *National Business Ethics Survey 2005: How employees view ethics in their organization (1994-2005)*. Arlington, VA: Ethics Resource Center. Retrieved from http://www.ethics.org/nbes2003/

Fuentes, S. C. G. (2008). *The link between learning culture and organizational performance in organizations using the balanced scorecard.* (Doctoral dissertation). Retrieved from ProQuest Dissertations and Theses. (Order No. 3346589)

Greenlee, J. S., & Bukovinsky, D. (1997). Protection from the federal sentencing guidelines. *The CPA Journal, 67*(8), 32-36. Retrieved from http://www.proquest.com/

Greenlee, J., Fischer, M., Gordon, T., & Keating, E. (2007). How to steal from a nonprofit: Who does it and how to prevent it. *Nonprofit Quarterly.* Retrieved from: http://www.nonprofitquarterly.org/2007

Hellman, S. W. (2000). *An evaluative study of the impact of new employee orientation on newcomer organizational commitment.* (Doctoral dissertation). Retrieved from ProQuest Dissertations and Theses. (Accession Order No. AAT 9962339)

Houlihan, D. (2015). Estimating the business impact of employee engagement in compliance and ethics training. *Blue Hill Research, 0143*, 1-7. Retrieved from http://www.bluehillresearch.com/estimating-the- business-impact-of-employee-engagement-in-compliance-and-ethics-training/

Johnson, K. (2004). Federal sentencing guidelines: Key points and profound changes. Retrieved from http://www.ethics.org/?q=resource/federal-sentencing-guidelines-key-points-profoud-changes/

Kaplan, R. S., & Norton, D. P. (1996). The balanced scorecard: Translating strategy into action. Boston, MA: Harvard Business School Press.

Kaplan, R. S., & Norton, D. P. (1992). The balanced scorecard: Measures that drive performance. *Harvard Business Review, 70*(1), 71-79.

Lee, C. (2014). *The adoption of outcome measures in nonprofit organizations: Empirical analysis of human service nonprofits.* (Doctoral dissertation). Retrieved from ProQuest Dissertations and Theses. (Order No. 3690308)

MacKessy, J. (2010). Knowledge of good and evil: A brief history of compliance. *The Finance Professional's Post.* Retrieved from http://www.nyssa.org/nyssa-news/2010/05/a-brief-history-of-compliance/

Mensch, S. (2007). *Evaluating governmental and corporate ethics policies and their effect on employees and upper management.* (Doctoral dissertation). Retrieved from ProQuest Dissertations and Theses. (Order No. 3241782)

Paine, L. (2003). Value shift. *Business Ethics Quarterly, 14*(4), 781.

Perkins, M., Grey, A., & Remmers, H. (2014). What do we really mean by "balanced scorecard"? *International Journal of Productivity and Performance Management, 63*(2), 148-169. doi:10.1108/IJPPM-11-2012-0127

Rutowski, K. D., Guiler, J. K., & Schimmel, K. E. (2009). Benchmarking organizational commitment across nonprofit human services organizations in Pennsylvania. *Benchmarking, 16*(1), 135-150. doi: 10.1108/14635770910936568

Sabir, M. S., Iqbal, J. J., Rehman, K. U., Shah, K. A., & Yameen, M. (2012). Impact of corporate ethical values on ethical leadership and employee performance. *International Journal of Business and Social Science, 3*(2). Retrieved from http://www.proquest.com/

Schmidt, S. W., & Akdere, M. (2007). Measuring the effects of employee orientation training on employee perceptions of vision and leadership: Implications for human resources. *The Business Review, Cambridge, 7*(1), 322-327. Retrieved from http:/www.proquest.com/

Shelton, K. (2010). *A quality scorecard for the administration of online education programs: A Delphi study.* (Doctoral dissertation). Retrieved from ProQuest Dissertations and Theses. (Order No. 3423965)

Steinholtz, R. (2015, January). The ends do not justify the means: Performance management and ethics. *Compliance & Ethics Professional,* 41-44.

Symonds, W.C. (2002). Tyco: How did they miss with a scam so big? *Bloomberg Daily Newsletter.* Retrieved from http://www.bloomberg.com/news/articles

Thomas, W. (2002). The rise and fall of Enron: When a company looks too good to be true, it usually is. *Journal of Accountancy.* Retrieved from http://www.journalofaccountancy.com/issues/2002/apr/therisandfallofenron

Thompson, K. R., & Mathys, N. J. (2008). The aligned balanced scorecard: An improved tool for building high performance organizations. *Organizational Dynamics, 37*(4), 378. Retrieved from http://www.proquest.com/

Trevino, L. & Nelson, K. (2007). *Managing business ethics* (4th ed.). Hoboken, NJ: Wiley.

United States Sentencing Commission. (2008). *Guidelines manual.* (2014, November). *Guidelines manual.* Retrieved from http://www.ussc.gov/guidelines-manual/guidelines-manual/

Valentine, S., & Johnson, A. (2005). Codes of ethics, orientation programs, and the perceived importance of employee incorruptibility. *Journal of Business Ethics, 61*(1), 45-53. doi:10.1007/s10551-005-7057-x

Weaver, G., Trevino, L., & Cochran, P. (1999). Corporate ethics programs as control systems: Influences of executive commitment and environmental factors. *Academy of Management Journal, 42*(1), 41-57. Retrieved from http:www.proquest.com/

Yang, C., Cheng, L., & Yang, C. W. (2005). A study of implementing balanced scorecard (BSC) in non-profit organizations: A case study of private hospital. *Human Systems Management, 24*(4).

Zimmerman, J. (2009, May). Using a balanced scorecard in a non-profit organization. *Nonprofit World, 27*, 10-12. Retrieved from http://www.proquest.com/

2

WHY DOES INTEGRITY MATTER?

Integrity is the most respectable part of human behavior and an important part of a company's value. Achieving sustainable success is impossible without integrity. So, what makes a person with integrity unique and different from others without it? What role does integrity play within a leadership context? According to Warren Buffet, three characteristics to look for in a person are energy, intelligence, and integrity. However, if a person lacks the third one, which is integrity, the other two do not matter. Integrity is not something that is learned in school, you were not born with it. It is simply up to you.

Integrity is being true to the social context in which you operate, being true to yourself. It's about your actions matching your words, and for those words to be true. Integrity is about being transparent, not about good or bad. Integrity is about standing by your words and your belief. It does not matter if others disagree or agree, whether they are watching or not. As human beings, we should all strive to be vessels of honor.

I believe everything that happens in nature is for good reasons and without secret ambitions. Although the outcome may not always be what we expect, it is honest, open and consistent because nature makes no moral judgments like humans. Whatever moral and/or ethical issue(s) surface, you must act with integrity.

People with integrity do not mistreat others; they treat them with respect and dignity whether or not it is deserved. My experience has taught me that a person's integrity cannot be known without observing them in different situations, e.g. including good or bad times, when they are with friends or strangers, or whether they are in public or behind closed doors. People with integrity can draw others close due to their being dependable and can be trusted. How you treat people who are unable to do anything for you is character.

The strength of a company depends on its integrity; trust will ensue when there is a high level of integrity. Trust is the foundation of every successful organization. The progress of an organization will be slow if integrity is lacking because much time will be spent on guarding one's interest and second-guessing others – time which could have been spent on how to make the organization more productive. Wasting time will enable competitors to conquer market share. An organization where there is a high level of integrity is often progressive and productive.

The responsibility of every member of an organization is to establish an uncompromising integrity, which is also the responsibility of its leaders. Ask yourself questions that will lead you to inculcate the habit of being honest in everything you do. As Don Miguel Ruiz recommends:

"Be concise with your words and speak with integrity. It is important to only say what you mean. Also, avoid using the word to speak negatively against yourself or to gossip about others. Use the power of your words in the direction of truth and love."

Remember to be a vessel of honor. Integrity matters, so be your word!

— Dr. Robyn

INTEGRITY IN A BUSINESS: WHY DOES IT MATTER?

Integrity matters a lot in our professions and our lives. Integrity communicates how we live our lives, and as well the values we hold. According to research, one of the fundamental traits employees, executives, and team leaders embrace in a workplace is integrity. Recruiters look for traits of integrity when hiring new employees because it communicates great moral and ethical principles vital for a healthy work culture and to inspire employee engagement.

DOES INTEGRITY MATTER IN A WORKPLACE?

Yes, it does. Individuals with integrity are guided by standards and values that enhance a good relationship with customers, colleagues, managers, and board members. Additionally, these persons respect others in the workplace and will only engage in appropriate behaviors and conversations. When employees have integrity, they do their job and perform responsibilities within the scope of the employee engagement. They understand work is work and personal is personal; the two never compete when placed in proper perspective.

Examples of integrity are the consistency of character, honesty, and dependability. Integrity enables individuals to be accountable either for what they will do or what they say. They do not violate the rules and regulations of the company; they take responsibility for their mistakes. People with integrity draw others close because they are dependable and can be trusted. People can count on them and they are principled in honorable ways whether they are alone or not.

You should be able to inspire others as a business leader. When it is demonstrated you can go beyond what is expected of you, it shows others that you embrace the conviction to make a difference, clear goals, and purpose. Work can be challenging; your employees may need reassurance that management not only backs their efforts but also practices the same trait. Integrity matters and it's very important in developing an organization.

3

WHAT IS COMPLIANCE & HOW TO USE THIS BOOK

Compliance program is referred to as an integrity or ethics program and represents an organization's commitment to adhere to all laws, regulations, internal policies and procedures that govern their business.

Ethical culture – more on this later in the book when companies teach their employees *"how things are done around here."* It begins with a code of conduct that is well-conceived, written, and effectively implemented.

A compliance officer is the face of compliance. They are the person who oversees and monitors an organization's compliance program. They help to assure that organizations or companies comply with all the rules and regulations that govern their business.

They are part of the team. Often, people think that it is the compliance officer's job to do everything that is related to compliance in the organization. However, a compliance officer is just one person, it takes the ENTIRE company to realize that everyone plays an essential role in compliance. A successful Compliance program requires that everyone does their part, EVERYONE from the president of an organization all the way down to the janitorial staff.

I always teach the above concept regarding compliance, especially when I go into organizations and companies to work, complete an assessment on the culture, and see where leadership fits into the equation. When leadership is not on board with compliance, more than likely, other levels of the management staff won't be serious about it either. The question becomes, "How committed to compliance is leadership?"

How does the senior leadership feel about compliance? There were times I have been in organizations where the top leadership told me: "*We are only doing this because we have to.*" That is the wrong attitude to have because the rest of the organization can sense the indifference and may adopt that way of thinking as well.

Top leadership sets the tone. YOU, leadership, set the tone for the rest of the ENTIRE organization. You set the tone for the culture, you set the tone for the atmosphere. So, if you are NOT serious about fraud not happening in your organization, or you are turning your face away and are not interested in establishing programs, policies, guidelines and even disciplinary measures to address the issues, wrongdoing, and fraudulent behavior, then employees will say: "Then why should I do the right thing? We have reported so many issues to upper management and nothing was ever done. Or the senior vice president knows that this guy over here is sexually harassing Susie in accounting, but nothing is being done about it. Why should I report what I saw?" It is better to get on board with compliance, do the right thing, set the tone, the expectations, and follow through.

Lead by example. I always say to an organization's leadership: "You are going to pay now, or you are going to pay later." Sometimes leadership views compliance as one more expense because they may not see the immediate return on investment (ROI). For starters, they might think administering compliance yields additional costs. When correctly implemented, there will be some costs. Take for example education, you must train your staff if you want them to perform well and avoid making costly mistakes.

Let's say a company is in the healthcare business, or maybe a Human Services Organization and they are getting monies from the government to provide a service. If they are billing the government for their services, usually the government will have criteria in place that requires an organization to have backup information/documentation for every product or service provided to bill them. If the documentation is not there, then the government/agency or funder will say the product or service was not provided. In those cases, this could trigger an audit. The government or agency funder might initiate an audit. When the compliance officer conducts an internal audit, the ethical and right thing to do, would be to send the money back to the government/funder when the organization can't substantiate that the product or service was provided.

When a compliance officer or compliance professional conducts an internal audit and cannot locate required documentation that supports a service was rendered, they know the company more than likely won't do well during an external audit. Why wouldn't an organization, once they have the right protocols, policies, and procedures in place, assure that things are being done properly so they could keep the money for the services they provide? Let's face it, most of these organizations can't afford to provide free services, and essentially that's what they are doing when they have to pay money back for a service they have already provided because they don't have the documentation to prove it. Why wouldn't leadership want to establish policies, procedures, and protocols to strengthen their internal systems to ensure they comply with laws and regulations?

START-UPS OR A COMPANY JUST STARTING OUT, OR JUST INCORPORATED. WHY WOULD THEY BENEFIT FROM READING THIS BOOK?

The reason the leadership at a start-up company should read this book is that it serves as a guide for instruction on establishing a robust compliance program; it explains why compliance is important, includes case studies, and best practices.

Additionally, the book will help start-ups avoid pitfalls. Why? Because if you are a new business owner, you may not know where to go for assistance. For example, you may be unaware that joining a trade association and finding people in your industry or network can be enlightening and beneficial.

I recommend new compliance professionals find mentors because it can feel lonely at times. Compliance officers are not always well received or appreciated in organizations. Some employees think that compliance officers are out to get them, e.g. when a compliance issue(s) is exposed, and disciplinary actions are taken, employees blame the compliance professional (who is only doing his/her job).

Most industries have trade and professional associations that compliance professionals can join to keep abreast of the latest happenings, such as cutting-edge technology, new laws and/or regulations, and any laws that may have changed. There are many benefits to having access to this information, including the ability for the compliance officer/professional to know what should be communicated to their senior leadership and other members of management. For example, a new legal requirement may surface, and the organization may be required to educate their employees on the change(s) and document that the training took place.

When organizations must change business practices because of a mandatory law, regulation or requirement, having access to trade associations, mentors, and connections will assist the compliance officer/professional on how to implement the change(s) correctly. Staying abreast and current on the latest requirements is crucial in compliance; make sure when that is your role as a compliance officer and compliance professional, you are on top of changes and updates in your respective industry.

After many years as a compliance professional, I am surprised by the number of people unfamiliar with the professional and trade associations in their industry, and/or have not thought about joining one to be informed, network, or advocate for change. Most industries have a professional trade association. If you are a coach, maybe you should join the International Coach Federation (ICF). Writers should get a Writer's Digest magazine subscription or attend the annual Writer's Digest Conference.

Another great resource is a subscription to newsfeeds for your industry; you can choose how often you receive updates, e.g. daily or weekly. The Society for Corporate Compliance and Ethics is an association that can benefit all compliance professionals in addition to compliance magazines and websites that are industry-specific.

Subscribe to popular industry-specific blogs; consider subscribing to blogs in your industry from key people who are known as experts. Consider bloggers/writers that keep a close eye on your industry. I receive blog posts every day from the **Foreign Corrupt Practices Act** (FCAP) blog. Why? I can see what's happening on an international level because I'm interested in international compliance. I can quickly see what is going on in any industry, for example, I like to know when a company is under scrutiny for potential wrongdoing and how much money they have to pay back as part of the FCPA settlement. The FCPA blog reports the number of companies that have disclosed open FCPA-related investigations.

Also, the FCPA blog reports on whistle-blowing, the number of cases there are, and the number of people convicted. Having access to this information can benefit organizations (think potential mergers and acquisitions. More on that later). "Knowledge is power." The information can be used for training and educational purposes. Additionally, the information can be used to update policies and procedures – knowing what others did wrong can motivate an organization to review and change their own practices/processes.

Let's talk about religious organizations such as church/faith-based organizations. This is an area where we have seen major compliance issues throughout the years. When I started my business, I did research on the church/faith-based organizations. I recall saying to myself: "I do not know of a church/faith-based organization that has a formal compliance and integrity program." I knew I had to write about the importance of compliance and integrity within these organizations and educate them about the potential pitfalls of not having a proper Compliance program in place.

The church/faith-based organizations are a unique entity because the leadership, often, is strong and controlling. This includes the pastor/leader, deacons, board of elders, and all those that make up the leadership in the organization. My experience with these organizations has been: "You are not going to tell us what to do." The leadership often wants to control everything; therefore, introducing and bringing compliance and integrity to church/faith-based organizations is difficult. My late uncle, who was a pastor, was open and receptive to implementing a Compliance program because he trusted me and understood as I explained to him why it was essential to have a program in place.

In this section, I address why compliance audits are not only nice-to-haves but MUST haves for church/faith-based organizations. I review the essential elements and specific areas to keep in mind when starting/updating the organization's audit system/process.

NON-PROFITS AND CHURCH/FAITH-BASED ORGANIZATIONS AUDITS

For this book, a church/faith-based* organization audit is defined as assuring fiscal integrity and stewardship are being performed to manage and monitor accounting of funds with other assets of the organization. Additionally, this section introduces the term Church Check-up Assessment in place of "check the books."

THE INTERNAL REVENUE SERVICE (IRS) AND CHURCH AUDITS:

The IRS, church audits and Freedom from Religion Foundation (FFRF) have been engulfed in controversy for nine years since 2009. This conflict occurred when a Minnesota church efficaciously challenged the IRS on its auditing churches procedures. The judge presiding over the case ruled in the church's favor. The court order now requires the IRS to modify their church audit methodology. Then in 2012, the FFRF challenged the IRS's alleged "preferential treatment of churches" in court. In 2014, the FFRF dropped their lawsuit after the IRS promised to resolve their internal policies. This included ending blanket policies and stopping the practice of non-enforcement of political activity.

The outcome between the IRS and FFRF requires church administrators to guarantee their organization's compliance. This can be done by conducting internal church assessments engaging a specialized compliance consultant, experienced church member, or volunteer. Additionally, compliance can be demonstrated via an external church audit when engaging a competent accounting firm.

CHURCH/FAITH-BASED ORGANIZATION AUDIT BENEFITS:

There are two kinds of audits:

- **External:** Carried out by an outside CPA or auditing firm.
- **Internal:** Carried out by individuals within the organization who understand fiscal management (often also aided by a specialized compliance consultant) and are not related to the individual handling the church's financial activities.

Audits are the best approach to:

- Assure all individuals responsible for fiscal management integrity are protected from baseless accusations of improper management of funds;
- Acquire financial donors' confidence and trust that their money is being used for the greater good.
- Establish protocols that ensure fiscal responsibility and management will continue if key-employees or clergy staff resign or pass away.
- Ensure that a donor's special instructions are implemented when they designate how the funds are to be dispersed or distributed by the church.
- Deliver checks and balances for money received and spent.

A Non-profit or Church Audit Should:

- Authenticate the accountant's report independently;
- Monitor funds and ensure their proper handling; and

- Create documents which substantiate that funds have been used as the donors specified.

The Auditor Monitors the Funds Going Through the System and Evaluates:

- **Accounting controls:** Methods that lessen the likelihood of loss or mistakes;
- **Segregation of duties:** Guarantees the involvement of more than one individual in managing funds to create checks and balances;
- Rationality of methods and processes considering all factors, and the magnitude of the organization and its budget;
- Status and suitability of insurance coverage; and
- Records that prove donors' instructions for the use of donations given to the organization.

Documents to Have Available:

A number of documents should be available when performing an internal or external audit. These are:

- Photocopies of the organization's policies, procedures, and processes associated with finance and all bank account functions including photocopies of documentation validating the approval of those policies.
- List of every bank, investment account along with the authorized individual(s) permitted to sign on each, and any special accounts used by the pastor(s) or administrators for non-profits or churches/faith-based organizations.

- Complete financial statements for every month of every year, including the December of the previous year and January of the following year, which is a fourteen-month time span.
- Bank and investment account statements for that same time span.
- Bank reconciliations for that same time span.
- Original books of entry, which are the general and subsidiary journals. For computerized books, a print-out of every transaction of a complete year (12-month period).
- All paid invoices, payroll data, and files of Employer's QUARTERLY Federal Tax Return form 941, year-end Wage and Tax Statement form

  W-2, Miscellaneous Income form 1099, income transmit-tals, transmittal forms, and deposit records for the audited period.

- The financial staff's records and additional income records for the same time span.

INTERNAL AUDITS

Both a non-profit and church/faith-based organization's internal audit process comprises auditing procedures executed by people within the organization; a specialized compliance consultant can be engaged to review internal protocols/processes. Internal audits can be cost effective as they do not include the expenses or costs of a full scope audit conducted by a CPA or Accounting Firm. In addition, an internal assessment or audit, can ensure that an organization's system of internal controls is functioning as planned. An internal auditor creates an audit program and schedule. It is highly recommended that churches/faith-based organizations and non-profits engage a CPA and/or an experienced compliance consultant who understands auditing and can help the organization to establish an internal audit program with training internal auditors.

Internal Auditor Qualifications:

An individual "qualified" to carry out an internal non-profit or church/faith-based organization audit should have experience related to accounting principles, all laws and regulations specific to the entity and its business, and office management. Additionally, the internal auditor should have high moral and ethical standards, a good reputation in the community, and understand the importance of confidentiality.

CONSIDERATIONS FOR PERFORMING A CHURCH/FAITH-BASED ORGANIZATION ASSESSMENT

All churches/faith-based organizations should incorporate church/faith-based organization assessments into their routine standard business practices. This initiative allows potential risk(s), misconduct, and any other problems to be discovered and mitigated right away. The parameters of a church/faith-based Organization Assessment can be defined mutually by the church, Certified Public Accountant (CPA), and/or a compliance consultant. Understand the purpose of the assessment is not to replace an audit conducted by an external accounting firm or the church/

faith-based organization's accountant. The assessment should be a proactive method for routine monitoring.

Depending on the church/faith-based organization, the assessment could include some or all of the following:

- Separation of duties
- Compensation and employment controls (*including Pastoral housing allowance and 1099 contractors*)
- Financial reporting controls
- Budgetary Controls
- Physical controls of building access
- Relevant computer files
- General controls (*minutes, insurance, etc.*)
- Cash controls
- Other items of importance to the church/faith-based organization

Since the church/faith-based organization defines the scope of work, a multi-year plan is sometimes developed where all topics are addressed over time. This provides a cost-controlled way to address the governing board's fiduciary responsibility. Additionally, there are several ways that church/faith-based organization boards can exercise their fiduciary responsibilities; both audits and assessments are necessary.

TIPS FOR CONDUCTING AN INTERNAL COMPLIANCE AUDIT

An internal compliance audit is an organization's system for reviewing its compliance with applicable legal and regulatory requirements within a designated time frame.

To execute internal audits that won't fail because of inefficiency requires a combination of both art and science. This isn't a "one size fits all" exercise as internal audits are structured in range of operations and the frequency is based on an organization's needs, resources, background history, and risk levels. It's highly recommended that every organization conduct a comprehensive internal compliance audit at least once per year.

The internal compliance audit process can satisfy various objectives. For example, a compliance auditor can ascertain the productivity of an organization's operations and the relevance of its policies and procedures. Concurrent internal compliance audits can be used as a method for mitigating risks and as an effective way of avoiding surprises during third-party audits that could originate in government agencies, insurance companies, and auditing firms, etc.

GENERAL CONSIDERATIONS IN CONDUCTING INTERNAL COMPLIANCE AUDITS

For a heightened level of efficiency during an internal compliance audit, these guidelines should be considered:

* Acquire buy-in for audits from the board of directors and top management officials of the organization, while ensuring such endorsements embrace and encourage transparency.

- Don't ignore contending priorities. It's not ideal to carry out an internal compliance audit while other third-party audits or other large and previously scheduled projects requiring a specified timeframe is demanding staff time and attention.

- Ensure the auditing process is comprehensive. Staff should be kept informed on the intent and consequences it may have on their respective department. Staff should also be given an assurance that information shared with the audit team is laudable and is in the best interest of the organization. This is necessary because most departments/staff that are constantly being audited view audits as stumbling blocks, threats, and a hassle.

- Employ a systematic method that makes sense and will not reduce the capacity of the Compliance program. There should be an audit plan, including both auditing and monitoring functions, that is achievable. The organization (assisted by an experienced compliance consultant) can map out strategies for its success, which can facilitate support for compliance exercises and initiatives.

RECOMMENDED INTERNAL COMPLIANCE AUDIT STEPS

1. **Know the credentials and expertise of individual(s) responsible for conducting the audit(s).**

    For starters, the organization's leadership should exercise due diligence and make sure the selected auditor or audit team has the appropriate qualifications regardless of whether the person or firm is internal or external. Members of the team must have the prerequisite knowledge and experience to perform a thorough audit. An auditor must be able to offer a considerable level of both internal and external audit experience. The ideal audit team should comprise both outside experts and internal staff. While external people may bring a noble perspective to the table including objectivity and professional competencies (and, if possible, the protection of the attorney-client communication privilege), they often relieve potential stress experienced by an organization's staff during the auditing process. It would be prudent for organizations with limited resources to vet external experts and firms because some charge exorbitant fees and may not have adequate experience or expertise.

Internal staff may be more effective than outside experts due to their existing knowledge of the organization's operations. It is possible for internal staff to have issues that may jeopardize the audit; this may include: lacking the required time and competencies needed for a proper audit or difficulties overcoming conflicts of interest that arise while auditing their own departments and/ or their colleagues.' Considering these potential inequalities, some organizations prefer to convene an audit team comprising both internal and external experts.

2. Ascertain the Scope of the Audit

Before starting the audit process, it is imperative the audit team understand an organization's expectations. Sometimes, the leadership may want the audit team to do more with limited resources. A comprehensive audit of the entire organization may seem impossible or unlikely. Until an organization can conduct a comprehensive audit, the focus should be on the departments with the highest risk.

Identifying and prioritizing the risk areas in an organization is called **risk assessment**. During developing and completing a risk assessment, the organization should review the findings and recommendations of previous internal and external audits. It would be pertinent to include important risk areas previously identified by state and federal regulatory and enforcement agencies.

Consulting with an organization's leadership can assist in identifying future loopholes in operations as the audit progresses. It will further enable the audit team to identify individuals in the organization with viable information that will allow the team to capitalize on resources instead of reinventing the wheel.

When a risk area is identified, the audit team should endeavor to create the scope to guide the audit. For example, take a non-profit human services organization that audits claims billed to their payors and/or insurance company; however, the scope is limited to only behavioral health claims. The non-profit human services organization may opt to audit its billing to all payors but limit the scope to a distinct time frame or type of service.

3.   Create an Audit Plan

Having established a range for auditing, the audit team can subsequently make a draft of the audit protocol to guide the process. A written audit plan should include the following:

1.   Scope of the audit
2.   The area to be audited
3.   Start and target end date
4.   List of auditors

5. Audit methodology. This element should include: (a) Description of audit procedure(s), (b) Description of the standards to be met, and (c) Sample size (if applicable)
6. A list of documents to be reviewed (if applicable)
7. A list of individuals to be interviewed (if applicable).

In creating the audit plan, it is imperative the audit team produces a sample with a size sufficient to establish a statistically valid sample. The team must also agree on whether the sample, e.g. ten consumer files, should be randomly selected based on the audit scope. Additionally, it is necessary that the audit parameters are goal-oriented, documented, and understandable. Standards that are not feasible may compromise the authenticity and acceptance of the audit results. Again, engaging an experienced compliance consultant early in the auditing process could help non-profits and churches/faith-based organizations with this process.

4. Document and Report Results

Organizations should develop a system to report and review concerns identified in the internal compliance audit findings. While some audits are not government–directed and are part of an organization's risk assessment and audit protocol, the results of internal audits may not be protected under attorney-client privilege. The organization should be certain the state requirements include guidance on the nature of information to be excluded, and safety measures to protect against compromising or corrupting the process.

5. Make Changes, Follow-up, and Re-audit

By conducting an internal compliance audit and/or assessment, organizations are one step closer to ensuring compliance with new regulations. An audit identifies risk areas; it is up to an organization's leadership to lessen the impact of those risks, by putting new controls and/or processes in place. Using the same audit scope, the processes must be routinely tested by conducting concurrent audits after implementation. The organization can keep track of the risk level; if a significant improvement is not observed, the organization can continue to try different approaches to mitigate these risks.

HANDLING CONTRIBUTIONS

Any non-profit organization should track and manage contributions to ensure accuracy. In 2006, a Pension Protection Act was passed which has altered the deduction rules for charitable contributions. Before this act was enforced, check registers or personal notations could be considered as reputable documentation. After the act passing, every donation must be documented via a donation receipt or bank record; a bank record can be a credit card statement, credit union statement, or a canceled check. The records must include the date of payment or when the payment posted, the payment amount, and the charity's name.

A donor cannot claim a tax deduction for any single contribution of $250 or more unless the donor obtains written acknowledgment of the contribution from the recipient organization (IRS Publication 1771).

WRITTEN ACKNOWLEDGMENTS FOR CONTRIBUTIONS:

The IRS Publication 1771 states that a *donor* is responsible for obtaining a written receipt from a charity for contributions totalling more than $250 before the donor claims the deduction on their federal income tax return. But the IRS necessitates a charity organization to give a disclosure in writing to a donor who accepts goods or services in return for a distinct payment greater than $75. A church/faith-based organization's policy should state whether they will provide donors with statements/receipts showing contributions, and/or make them accessible to those who request them.

REQUIREMENTS FOR A CONTRIBUTION RECEIPT:

The receipt should consist of the church/faith-based organization's or non-profit's name, amount(s), the date(s) of the donation(s) and the donor's name. It is necessary to include a statement indicating if the charity has delivered any goods or services to the donor. If nothing was delivered, then the organization can note it as follows:

"You did not receive any goods or services in connection with these contributions other than intangible religious/faith-based benefits."

A yearly contribution statement will fulfill this condition for churches.

Organizations should ensure that donors are given copies of all receipts before the date of their tax return filing. If the organization has a policy to provide receipts yearly, they must provide all receipts to donors by January 31st at the latest.

Frequency:

An organization can determine how often it provides donation receipts. However, if they have a policy and procedure manual, the frequency should be documented in the policy and/or procedure manual.

Form:

There are no laws or regulatory requirements stating what a donor receipt should look like except for gifts including boats, automobiles, or airplanes. In these instances, the Contribution of Motor Vehicles, Boats, and Airplanes Form 1098-C should be used. The receipt can be in a postcard, computer-generated form or a letter. The IRS does not require a donor's social security number or extra taxpayer identification number be included on receipts; and the receipt can be sent electronically.

Report and Value:

A written receipt should be provided for every non-cash contribution. It's not an organization's responsibility to create value of non-cash items nor do they need to place value on receipts. A law passed in 2004 which required additional documents for qualified vehicles, including airplanes, automobiles, and boats.

Gifts:

When pastors, church/faith-based organizations employees, or needy individuals receive a gift from church/faith-based organization's members, the gift itself is not eligible for a charitable contribution deduction and it should not be included on a donor's annual contribution statement.

DONATED LABOR AND SERVICE CONTRIBUTION:

The IRS doesn't allow tax deductions specifically for donated services or labors; a receipt for donated materials and other out-of-pocket expenses can be issued. A volunteer's unreimbursed expenses for volunteer work can be reported on their personal income tax return.

Important note: *If a volunteer's expenditures are greater than $250, they must be given a letter specifying the services(s) delivered. The letter must exclude the value of volunteer's expenditures. It is a volunteer's responsibility to justify and substantiate their expenses.*

To summarize, maintain accurate and precise records of contributions. Whichever method the organization employs to keep track of the contributions, it must incorporate a policy stipulating a timeframe for providing receipts to donors.

INTERNAL CONTROLS

Internal controls are measures utilized by an organization to safeguard assets from waste, fraud, and inefficient use. Internal cash controls can be a sensitive issue in churches/faith-based organizations or non-profits, especially those that rely on volunteers.

An organization should be built on the concepts of honesty, integrity, and mutual trust. Having internal controls not only protect the organization's interests but can protect staff members from false allegations and misunderstandings. Most volunteers and church/faith-based organization staff members are good honest people and do not mind controls put into place that protect the organization's assets from theft or loss.

ESTABLISHING INTERNAL CONTROLS

Because each church/faith-based organization or non-profit is unique and operates with its own set of unique circumstances, the financial leaders of each organization must design a system of internal controls to meet their specific needs. Accountants, and compliance professionals, have the knowledge and expertise to help churches/faith-based organizations and non-profits implement these needed procedures.

INTERNAL CONTROL PROCEDURES:

Based on my experience, the most important measure organizations can put in place is a separation of duties.

Three basic types of financial activities are performed in a church/faith-based organization or non-profit:

1. Authorization of transactions
2. Recording of transactions
3. Custody of assets

Due to limited resources, it is not uncommon for small churches/faith-based organizations and non-profits to have only one person handling all of their financial affairs. However, leadership should try, if possible, to use enough individuals to properly segregate these activities...for that person's sake as well as the organization.

For a church/faith-based organization:

- Offerings should always be counted by at least two non-related individuals (regardless of how big or small the organization might be).
- Counters and ushers should be rotated periodically.
- Counters should have a safe room to count the offerings with no interruptions.
- Counters should fill out a count summary form and sign it with ink to verify their accounting.

Then a second individual should record the contributions to each family's or individual's contribution record, to the general ledger and then depositing the funds in the bank as soon as possible. The money should be kept in a safe until deposited. Third, another unrelated individual who has had no access to the funds should perform a bank reconciliation each month.

For a non-profit:

There are a wide range of internal controls. For example, an organization might have authorization lists indicating who can access different floors, offices, types of information, etc. All mail should be opened by one person who logs in each check received.

This person should be someone other than the person who deposits the checks in the bank. Disbursements of large amounts, for example over $500, may require a secondary signature.

FOR BOTH CHURCHES/FAITH-BASED ORGANIZATION AND NON-PROFITS:

The responsible person should verify that all checks have been properly signed and that the bank balance reconciles to the bookkeeping records. They should also verify that the beginning balance equals the ending balance of the previous month both in the checking account and the general ledger.

Another internal cash control procedure is establishing clear guidelines for handling the organization's funds along with conducting an annual financial audit. The audit may be external (performed by an outside CPA) and/or internal (reviewed by people in the organization who understand financial management).

Last, the organization should have a policy that indicates all checks require two signatures. Those writing and signing the checks should have the responsibility of checking all invoices for accuracy before payment is made.

Check Writing:

- Ideally, there should be three people who can sign church/faith-based organization checks in case of an emergency.
- The check stub copy of the check or the check number should be attached to the authorization and documentation (receipts, etc.) and filed for auditing purposes.

- The supporting document such as an invoice should be marked "Paid" to avoid overpayment.
- All blank checks should be stored in a safe or an office with a lockable door.

Deposits:

- All checks and cash should be processed immediately with all checks stamped, "For Deposit Only" before they are secured or deposited.
- Records must be kept so retrieval of the items deposited can be verified if there is a dispute over a deposit.
- Develop a numbering system to match deposit slips with computer records.

Handling church/faith-based organization or non-profit funds is an act of stewardship. A concerted effort should be made to assure the organization's resources are properly managed.

As you can see there are a lot of moving pieces and even more steps required for non-profit, churches/faith-based organizations' audit procedures and processes. I understand if the information above makes you feel both excited and nervous at the same time, but helped by a great CPA firm, accountant and/or experienced compliance consultant, your organization should be in good hands and more than prepared to perform the required audit obligations/responsibilities. I recommend leaders and organizations always consult with their current financial advisors or other relevant professionals when entertaining making changes/improvements to their current or new audit procedures.

*   Church/faith-based organizations
    A church or faith-based organization is an organization whose values are based on faith and/or beliefs, with a mission based on social values of the particular faith, and which most often draws its activists (leaders, staff, volunteers) from a particular faith group.

My uncle was an older gentleman, he died at seventy-nine. But at seventy-nine years old he had just built a new church. We marched into his brand-new church last March. When others were retiring, he was still building because he would always say: "God is not done with me yet." He wanted everything to be in order; he wanted the church's business to be in compliance.

With his church, I would tell him: "When you take up tithes and offerings, you must explain to the members that for the church to be able to provide them with a statement for tax purposes at the end of the year, they have to understand that they need to pay by check. The cash offering, they are used to putting in an envelope that indicates $5, $10, $20, etc. is not going to work anymore. They should write a check because that is their record/receipt. This method is for those members who want a year-end statement detailing the tithes and offering paid (charitable contributions)."

The cash tithing practice isn't practical anymore with the law, and the IRS. I had to explain those changes to him. I provided him with language to share, and to make sure the changes were communicated correctly to his church members.

Even with the allowances the church gave to him; if they paid for gasoline when he traveled, hotel expenses, a car, or whatever they paid for, all of that had to be documented so it did not leave room for violations or errors. I wanted to make sure he wasn't in violation of laws, even if he did not do it on purpose. In the past, pastors didn't have to report to the church's members. All the church's financial information was kept private, but as we see, the church has become a business, and the government wants to treat it as such. We saw what happened in the Catholic church a few years back. Where were the whistleblowers in the church, when these priests were allegedly doing illegal and heinous acts?

I can't help wondering what if there had been a toll-free number or someplace where people could have called or gone to and felt comfortable reporting anonymously what they knew without fear of retaliation. Perhaps the problem could have been discovered and stopped MUCH earlier. If the church had a compliance program that includes a code of conduct policies and procedures, and mandatory educational training the malfeasance could have been eliminated and prevented in most cases. What would make them think that moving priests from one parish to another would prevent the acts from been committed again? Moving troubled priests to other parishes instead of properly dealing with the situation was not an appropriate solution. They were just exposing other people, mainly children, to this wrongdoing. Could have, would have, should have, right? Unfortunately, the damage and abuse had been done.

Religious institutions are not exempt just because they are a church/faith-based organization, there are still tax laws they must know of, regulations and codes to follow, and then there is the ethics piece. This book deals with both ethics and integrity. Yes, there is the compliance piece but what about ethics and integrity?

There is a phrase I say a lot: *"Just because it's legal doesn't make it ethical."* We must look at ethics in our businesses and relationships; some things may be legal, but what about ethical? The actions or decisions that an employer takes may be legal but not ethical. An example might be firing an employee two months before they are eligible for retirement. This action might be legal; however, people may not consider it to be ethical.

I briefly mentioned a helpline to report misconduct, violations of code of conduct, etc. (for employees looking to report wrongdoing or suspicious activities). The question often comes up, "Where do the calls made to that number(s) end up?" It depends on the organization, its size, structure, and other factors. I have seen some companies have different setups depending on their size and geographical locations. Their helpline could be handled within the company or externally by an independent third party. I have worked with organizations whose headquarters are in the USA, and they have subsidiaries and employees all around the world.

Take, for example, Nabisco, General Mills, Hershey Foods, and other companies of similar size and type, they have locations all over the world. As such, they may have regional compliance officers/professionals in various countries. The helpline number can be directly routed to a person within a compliance department through a system. Based on an organization's policy on handling those calls along with special advancements in technology, calls can be recorded, not recorded, and/or might be handled by a third-party company or service provider. It is up to an organization to determine the appropriate process for handling the helpline and anonymous reporting.

Because some employees are afraid to call and feel: "If I call, they are going to find out who I am," corporations allow their employees to report anonymously. Allowing anonymous reporting may encourage employees to make good faith reports of potential or real issues. When a compliance officer has a reputation for being integral and trustworthy, employees may provide their complete name and contact information because they are not afraid of the repercussions. Their main interest is finding a resolution. A lot of companies provide many options for reporting violations.

With advancements in technology, companies have added portals or sites where employees can go online to make a report and remain anonymous if they choose. Still, the organization must be able to pledge to the employees that they make no effort to find out the identity of those that choose to use any reporting resources. They should say something like: "We are interested in what you are reporting, not who is doing the reporting." We are interested in your good faith efforts. It is important for the company to know what is being reported more than who is reporting the problem/issue. Many who oppose anonymous reporting debate the inability to follow up when additional information is required.

I have seen corporations shifting away from providing toll-free numbers for helplines. As mentioned, companies should provide diverse ways to report because some employees don't have access to computers, or they may prefer not to use a computer. Others would rather make a telephone call and report via that option. The compliance programs that work include many options for employees to report. Why? "Because the thing is, you want employees to report when they see something, to say something when they are aware of real or potential issues. Progressive organizations provide various ways for employees to feel comfortable making a decision to report, e.g. using a third-party vendor/agency.

Employees might consider external resources as safer ways to report because the service is provided outside their organization. "I feel like they don't know me. I don't know them either. I'll just report this issue to them instead of using the company's 1-800 number and I don't have to fear retaliation."

The hotline as it was initially called and referred to as helpline when I was in corporate America, came into my office. My executive assistant had access to the system and managed the voicemail. Our process was to let the calls go to voicemail and then follow up if the reporter requested a return call and provided their contact information. We didn't want employees to feel vulnerable or unsafe; they could report and not need to worry about someone judging them, disclosing their identity to upper management or to their manager.

My colleagues on the leadership team were desperate at times to find out the reporter's name. My response was, "No because it doesn't matter." Is what they said true? That's what we need to consider. Not all reports, including anonymous reports, are made in good faith. Some employees use the system to get back at a co-worker or their supervisor. Also, disgruntled employees may abuse the system by incessantly making reports. In these instances, it would be good to know who is abusing the system so action can be taken.

No fear of retaliation. In setting up a toll-free line or process in the church, or any other faith-based religious organization, all calls should be processed by an outside third party that can assure neutrality. Leadership should not be involved especially when the people monitoring the process are the bishop, pastor, priest, archbishop, or leader. The whistleblower may not want to report what they have seen or know because they view the leadership as powerful people and believe their report would disrupt the church/organization.

This is a reason I advocate for these organizations to have an independent third party handle all allegations; they will be able to address the concern(s) or potential issue(s) without preconceived ideas or judgments.

Remember, you might encounter people who are disgruntled, upset and may be inclined to embellish because of the way they were treated. It is important to ensure employees understand the term: *good faith effort.* We are interested in your good faith reports ONLY. Organizations are only interested in good faith reports, not those motivated by or based on revenge.

This book will help established organizations to assure that they are in compliance. There may be information an organization's leadership may not know of; the content provided should enable them to consider how to be in compliance. Compliance can be an overwhelming subject for those who have no background or understanding. My experience working in the industry suggest you either love it or you don't. For experienced professionals, the book can help them with creative ways to bring their team on board or to get buy-in from both their colleagues and leadership. They will also learn educational concepts I have discovered along my journey. I intend to share my knowledge to help compliance professionals and other leaders avoid pitfalls; in addition to bringing light to concepts and ideas they may have missed.

When companies or organizations plan or are in the process of expanding their business internationally, they MUST realize the importance of understanding a country's culture. Additionally, it is important to research, to have a complete understanding of the regulatory and legal requirements in other countries.

It's important for companies to know cultural differences when writing policies, especially when they have employees all over the world. Every employee may not or cannot subscribe to a company's American culture because some things, such as traditions, might be different in their home country and/or culture. In some countries, women aren't allowed to ride in the same car with a man not related to them. If you are a male executive traveling on business to certain countries in the Middle East, you must be aware that a woman is not getting in the same car even if she is your employee. The male executive may not be able to take a female out to lunch for a business meeting; it may not be their culture or their custom. Please remember that not all businesses function like the USA. It is necessary to become educated on the culture and the customs of the countries you want to do business with and understanding their laws are crucial.

For example, the USA has Health Insurance Portability and Accountability Act of 1996 (HIPAA). These laws provide data privacy and security provisions for protecting health care information. Other countries such as the United Kingdom (UK) have different privacy laws. They follow the General Data Protection Regulations (GDPR). In the UK, transmitting records about an employee over the internet can be problematic. Again, a company should exercise due diligence to know all laws and regulatory requirements in other countries. Management should ensure all know of the requirements. Otherwise, they could face consequences such as, paying fines and penalties or losing business, or customers.

MATERNITY LEAVE:

If you have employees in other countries who may take or use maternity leave, leave time they may be entitled to can be different than the Maternity Leave Policy in the USA. USA laws addressing the subject should be understood BEFORE the company hires employees. Sick leave and time off policies are different from USA policies. Do your research.

I hope that by reading this book you will understand the difference between compliance and ethics. I am an educator at heart and feel the amazing responsibility to share with others what I have learned along the way.

One of the many reasons I wanted to write this book was because I saw the positive impact having a well put-together Compliance program has on companies that have one and the negative impact on those that don't.

Hey, enjoy the ride and have fun, but know that no matter what stage your company is, you will benefit from reading this book. I promise this is an easy to read book for both compliance veterans and new people entering the field of compliance.

4

MY STORY:
HOW IT ALL BEGAN

My compliance journey started when I graduated from college. I did my undergraduate work at Syracuse University (SU). I went there with hopes of becoming a pediatrician. I was pre-med and everything I did educationally was pre-med. I was in all kinds of science and medicine-related programs in high school. I was admitted into a special program that allowed me to go into the operating room and see live operations being performed. I was so psyched about medicine; I took advantage of opportunities which included programs and everything medicine-related I could get into.

I was ecstatic about becoming a physician. I got to SU and went through all the normal stuff students go through, settling in, meeting new people, etc.

Everything was going according to plan until one day I began a class where we had to dissect things – I didn't mind dissecting frogs, I didn't mind the Guinea pig either, but when we got to animals like cats, and other things I could not. I just could not do it. Believe it or not, that was a stumbling block for me because even though I did not mind cutting into people – after all I had seen hysterectomies, tumors and gall bladders removed, etc. When I was in the operating room, I could handle it. But with cats; cutting a cat and other animals I could not; it bothered me, and I changed my concentration after that. I thought maybe I would revisit medicine, but I found myself leaning towards law – I was always good at arguing; great at defending, speaking too. "I'm going to do the law thing now; who knows, maybe one day I would become a doctor and a lawyer. I'll be one of those people who are both a doctor and an attorney." That's me, always having high hopes and expectations. I graduated from SU and got accepted to law school. I was on my way to law school.

I was this 21-year-old who thought I knew everything. After college graduating from SU, I moved back home, and that meant following the house rules again. I came from a very strict upbringing, and even though I was out of school, I still had to follow the rules of the house.

Don't get me wrong I wasn't rebellious or anything like that. I had the utmost respect for my parents, especially my mom; we were extremely close. I can truly say I was straight as they come; however, the mouthy thing was an issue for sure. I had a disagreement with my parents, and it did not help that they had told me they would not pay for me to go to law school.

Picture this, until the point it was time for me to go to law school, I thought they weren't going to pay for it, and I didn't have the means to pay for it. I decided that I would not go to law school. Approximately one week and a half before it was time for me to leave for school, my parents asked me: "So what day do we have to take you to school? When are you going?" I could not believe what I was hearing. I recall saying: "What are you talking about?" Of course, by then we had kissed and made up, and all was well. My parents were planning to pay for law school all along; I just did not know it. I was mad because all that summer I could've been making plans and preparing for the next chapter of my life. Me being who I am, determined to always move forward, I had already planned another strategy for my life.

What happened? I didn't go to law school because I was being stubborn, very stubborn and it cost me. I worked instead; I found a company that would pay for me to go to graduate school. I went to Pennsylvania State University (Penn State) for my master's degree.

Around this time, my mother became ill, and she ended up on dialysis; she had kidney failure. A lot of things were going on and I needed to be home to help take care of her. Had I gone away to law school I wouldn't have been able to focus on school. I would not have focused on any of my classes. I was home, and although we shared a great support system, that included my father, and two sisters, we were all needed. We loved our mother so much and endeavored to assure she had everything she needed and wanted.

We created schedules. I would take her to dialysis, somebody else would pick her up, or I would pick her up after her appointments. Unfortunately, she ended up having the toes on her right foot amputated. The amputation made it even more imperative I be home. It was good we were all around to support her and each other.

During this time, I was working for Pennsylvania Blue Shield – subsequently, it became Highmark Blue Shield – I worked in the

Professional Services Department; my position entailed training doctors and medical staff on Medicare and billing insurance laws. The position required significant traveling and anytime there were changes to the federal regulations and/or Federal Register, I went to my regions and conducted presentations and trainings. I developed personal relationships with medical societies, congressmen, congressional leaders and their staff, and constituents. I was out "in the field" trying to make a difference. Through the course of working in professional services, I became the expert on nephrology, which deals with the kidneys – the same disease my mom had – she had kidney failure, so I became the expert in my department on the subject. I met the top medical doctors including nephrologists in our state.

I developed a thorough understanding of the disease, the medications, prescribed for my mom to treat her and what she was experiencing. Having that knowledge enabled me to educate my family, including my mom. When things were being prescribed or suggested for her body, I knew what questions to ask her doctors and could explain what was going on with her. This proved to be a great benefit to my family. Mom truly was my best friend and she is the reason I am the professional and woman I am today.

My mother, who I affectionately called Mommy or Mindy Mom, was the first one that taught me about God and prayer. Eventually, my mom passed, I was still in graduate school at the time. I had finished all the coursework and the only thing left to complete the program was the thesis. However, I was succumbed by grief. I knew she was saved beyond a shadow of a doubt. I knew who she was, still, I was very grief-stricken. Heartbroken. My heart was just broken. I cried every day. I was like: "Is there ever going to be a day when I'm not shedding a tear over my mom?" I'm getting teary-eyed just talking about it and that was a long time ago, 1995 to be exact.

I did not want my master's program to be a waste of time. After all, I had finished all the coursework and the only thing left to do was to write the thesis. "Maybe I'll just go to law school now," I said to myself. But instead as fate would have it, I leaned more into my career. I left Highmark and went to work at United Concordia Companies, Inc. (UCCI), a wholly-owned subsidiary. I was recruited because of my noted speaking capabilities, education, and training, and knowledge of billing insurance companies. The top management was looking to start a compliance program. I could not believe it, I thought to myself: "Compliance, laws and regulations? This will help me as I considered applying to law school again. Yes, I'll do that." I started work at UCCI, and that's where it all started, officially anyway. What was I doing at Highmark? I was educating and training, it was all compliance. I was teaching employees, providers, legislators and their staff, and constituents, how to comply with laws and regulations.

Who would have thought, right? I started the job and loved it. Making sure that people understood all requirements and the "why" behind them, motivated me to learn more so I could give more.

As a Public Relations and Professional Services Representative at Highmark, Inc., I educated physicians and their office staff how to comply with laws, billing requirements, errors, and much more. I was doing the same for UCCI, only working with dentists.

Unlike my time at Highmark working closely with providers, I did not work with dentists as much. I spent more time in-house working with our staff, who were all over the country because we had offices in just about every state. My main goal was to educate staff, so they could not only be effective but also successful when servicing all customers. because we had offices in about every state. One day, I received a call from the Vice President of Human Resources (HR); he told me about a new position in National Marketing and said I was being recruited for the position. I believe the things that happen to us in life are intentional and coincidental. Guess what my undergrad major was at SU after I changed from Pre-med? I majored in Speech Communications and Marketing!

I have a passion for communications and marketing; however, compliance makes my heart beat a little faster. I said: "This is what I really love doing so why can't I mix the two? Why can't I do compliance and education because both are necessary?" While working in National Marketing at UCCI, my bosses were in Phoenix, Arizona and I was in Pennsylvania, so I would travel back and forth. Eventually, they wanted me to relocate to Phoenix. My response: "I don't think so. I like Phoenix, but I don't want to live there. I don't want to live in a desert; I need to have water like an ocean, river or lake close by me." Add to that my family situation with my dad was a major concern because my mom had passed away. We were a very close-knit family and I was concerned about my father. I believe it was not the right time to relocate.

Subsequently, an opportunity popped up to start a Compliance program for a human services organization. I looked at it, and I said to myself: "Oh, I don't know if I want to do that." The position kept coming across my mind; I couldn't shake it. Eventually, I inquired about the position ended up getting the interview, and the rest, as they say, is history. My primary focus with the new organization was developing their compliance department – they brought me in because they were in trouble, they needed compliance – they had to pay back money to a funder due to some major billing errors.

This organization needed a professional experienced in compliance and had certain skills and the ability to create a robust compliance and integrity program. I had the initial interview with the CEO; I had five interviews before I was offered the position. First, I met with the CEO, followed by a second interview with leadership, a third meeting with other key members of the senior leadership team, a fourth interview with the president, and the fifth and final interview with the board of directors. The interviewing process was draining but that was their process, at least for me.

I worked at that human services organization for many years. One day while sitting in my office, I realized I needed something more. I knew I loved what I was doing but something was missing. I thought about going back to school, even though the mere idea of it was frightening because I hadn't been in school for a long time. As mentioned, education has always been my passion. I will be a hundred years old and will be taking some classes. I don't care what type of class it is; it can be cooking or a computer class. No matter what, I have purposed in my heart to always learn something new. A post-card came in the mail and it referenced an opportunity at George Washington University. Since I'm always looking for ways to make sure that I remain on the cutting edge of the latest in my industry, going back to school felt like the next logical step.

After being out of college for many years, I applied for a graduate program at George Washington University in healthcare compliance. It was my introduction back into the education realm. The program was a hybrid because most of the curriculum took place online while the remainder of the time students were required to attend sessions on campus.

I had not completed the program when I felt that tug again: "It's time for you to go back to school." AGAIN! I said: "Well God, what do you want me to do? I'm almost done with this program and you want me to continue school. What else do you want me to do?" His answer: "It's time for you to get your doctorate degree." I did not even hesitate to say: "I'm not trying to do all that." The thought of writing a dissertation felt nearly impossible. I did not think I could do it. Perhaps my graduate program at George Washington stirred up something in me.

There was a woman in the admissions office when I was in graduate school at Penn State. She always supported me, pushed me, and encouraged me. After I graduated from Penn State, I would see her occasionally. Whenever we got together, she would always say: "We have a doctoral seat with your name on it at Penn State. One day you are going to do it. I just know it."

Her continuous encouragement motivated me to contact Penn State. I talked to some of my old professors who teach in the doctorate program I was considering. In the back of my mind, I didn't think I should have to take the Graduate Management Admission Test (GMAT) or the Graduate Record Exam (GRE) tests. I kept thinking: "Why? Why do I have to? I mean I already had a degree from Penn State." The thought of even studying for the "new math" stuff made me uneasy. I kept thinking: "There's no way I'm going to pass that test."

"I USED to be a math genius. I don't know how to do algebra anymore. I'm sorry; I don't know how to do this stuff." My monologue continued with: "I'd have to hire somebody just to coach me on how to do these math problems just so I could pass the GMAT or GRE. What if I fail the test, then what? It's not cheap to get a tutor or to take the test." I kept trying to convince the chair of the Department who knew me to waive the test requirement for me. His answer was not what I expected: "Robyn, I'm sorry, the rules are the rules; we have to comply with them. You have to take the GREs or other standardized tests."

My answer may not have been what he was expecting either: "I don't understand because this makes no sense. These standardized tests are not indicative of anyone's potential success or failure in school. You really need to eliminate this requirement." He gave me hope for a split second: "I agree, but until that time, my hands are tied, there's nothing I can do."

I had to decide, and I did not know what to do. Meanwhile, I found out that I would qualify for scholarships that were available. Receiving scholarships to pay for school was great; however, I was not happy with their pre-requisites.

I continued with my life until I would have to decide. Again, life is intentional. I was invited to speak at an event with the mayor of the city where I resided along with two other panelists. I spoke about corporate and social responsibility and corporate governance. There were hundreds of people in attendance and it was an awesome day. While socializing I met somebody after the event who works at Drexel University. We were conversing about my position on social responsibility when I heard that little voice inside saying: "I kept telling you to look at other places. It's Drexel." I never thought about Drexel until that very moment.

At first, I was thinking about the costs and wondered if Drexel had scholarships available. My employer at the time paid for my graduate studies at George Washington University but would not be paying for or contributing funds toward a Doctoral Program. I looked at Drexel's requirements. And lo and behold, at first glance, a standardized test was required. I continued reviewing all requirements and was about to give up when I felt something say: "Just call them." I called the university and I got connected to a gentleman in the Admissions Department. We talked about the potential dates for applying based on when I wanted to begin the program.

Everything was going well until we went over the requirements. I brought up my GRE reservations, and then I got on my soapbox. *"I don't think it's indicative of anyone's potential success or failure. I don't know why I have to take this test. I have this. I have years of experience, etc."* I recall speaking fast and was almost out of breath towards the end of my diatribe.

To my surprise, he said: "Are you done? Take a breath, just take a breath. Can I call you Robyn?"

I remember saying "Yes."

He said: "We have a pilot program right now because we think just like YOU think. And if you can get your application to us (within a ten-day time frame) and if everything else is in line and you qualify, meaning you meet all the other requirements, we will waive the requirement for a GRE test. This is pilot number two, and it is the last one." I could not say anything while I was taking in EVERYTHING he said.

I had ONLY ten-days to gather the prerequisites. I had to contact all my prior universities to obtain transcripts, write a paper indicating my "fit" for the program, submit a bio, resume, samples of my writing, and more. I made that deadline and ultimately was accepted into the program. Drexel is where I was supposed to get my doctorate degree all along. Did I get scholarship money? No, I had to pay out of pocket, but the benefit of getting into the program without taking the tests was amazing. My destiny caused me to meet some of the greatest people I know today. This is one of the main reasons I am so thankful for Dr. Kristen Betts. I learned a lot from her; she always connected me with people with similar interests and is still doing so to this day.

Drexel University is about an hour and a half drive by car, so I chose the online program where all my classes were virtual opposed to the Executive Program which required students to attend classes on campus besides online. I could attend classes on campus if I wanted, but why would I do that when I could take the classes from the comfort of my house. By design, the classes were kept small on purpose and generally, there were no more than 20-students per class. I felt I was in an actual classroom; we could see each other using the cameras on our laptops/computers. We had to attend all the classes just like in a traditional school setting.

In most of my courses, during the time I was completing the program, the last year to be exact, a few things happened with my employer that had me saying: "I can't do this anymore." I left the organization to focus on my dissertation and to care for my father who was experiencing medical complications. Then I started my own company, One Accord Consulting Firm. One goal was to have my own consulting firm someday. I did not think that *some day* would come so soon and for the reasons it came.

Everybody else in my life saw it before I did. Having my own company was something I desired to do for sure, but I did not expect to start earlier than my original plan. I felt this urgency to just do it as Nike says! The way things were going at my employer, I had to do it. I was stretched out of my comfort zone and I found myself in a place I had not been before. I was not working full-time, taking care of my father with medical issues, going to school, and living off my savings. I was very happy and didn't know why. I would say to myself, "This makes no sense, it just does not make sense." The fascinating thing was when I left my former employer, I had no regrets, and I never looked back.

One day I got an email from a consultant I used to work with on special projects, I don't even know how he got my personal email address, but he did. He tried contacting me at my prior employment but heard I was no longer working there. He said: "I was in a meeting yesterday and your ears should have been burning because I was talking about you. I need to talk to you right away about a consulting opportunity." We scheduled a time to talk, and there it all began.

"I'm working for myself I told him." He said: "You are the expert in this situation and we really need you because we don't have anybody on our team that can do this." As I was listening to him, I realized he was somebody I used to engage for the company I just left to do external consulting. I would contact him to audit and to assure specific programs and services complied with financial and regulatory requirements. I hadn't seen or talked to him in several years. We would email each other at times to check in and see how things were going. Whenever he was in the area, we would have lunch, but we had not done that in a while.

How funny is that? The company I used to hire as consultants became one of my clients. Prior to this opportunity, I had been consulting with other organizations on a limited basis. It had become official, I was an entrepreneur and my company grew by word of mouth, and some of the clients' attorneys refer their clients as well.

This is why I say when I talk to people about my business and the way God uses me in the marketplace: *"You have to be open and willing to allow God to direct you."* Often, we go to God in prayer, we ask God for things, but do we really want God to do what He wants to do in our lives? We may have a plan, but so does He. Let me apologize to those of you who do not subscribe to my faith and may be offended, I'm sorry. I don't mean to be preachy, but I apologize for the offense, but not for my conviction surrounding my faith. "Tell me what you would have me do next." God says in His word in Jeremiah 29:11 NIV: *"I know the plans that I have for you"* and you know the rest of how that verse goes: *"plans to prosper you and not to harm you, plans to give you hope and a future."* So, if He knows the plan, why am I trying to create my own?

Why wouldn't I be seeking His plan for my life? Because His way is perfect. That's what the Bible says. It took me a while to get there and the reason why was because I kept trying to do things my way and every time I got ahead of God, I messed it up. Sometimes His permissive will was there, but it wasn't His perfect will. So, I seek His will now and I begin my day with prayer at 6:00 AM. During my prayer time, I ask: "What will You have me do?" I want to do *everything* for Him in excellence. Even when I began this book project, I was trying to make it happen BEFORE the appointed time, and that was not God's plan. I clearly see why it was to be written when it was and not before it was time.

Again, He knows the plans He has for us and our future. If He said: "It's going to be easy," then it will be easy. You don't have to force anything. As I reflect, I thought 2017 was *the best* year of my life. Last year, 2017, was amazing for me and as I wrapped up the year, He told me, even before 2017 ended: "2018 is going to be even greater." I kept wondering: "How? How is that even possible, God?" Looking at the way 2018 has started, I'm not asking how anymore. Seriously, it has been complicated; there have been ups, and downs, however, I still trust God. The year may have begun hectic but it's not going to end that way because I trust God.

While speaking with friends and colleagues, they told me 2018 has been the same for them, hectic. There is a lot of ruffling around because – ruffling feathers, if you will – is an indication that things have to fall off.

I believe nothing about our process should feel rushed or intense. If it gets intense, it's because we may need to grow in some area of our life.

5

COMPLIANCE CONSULTANTS? WHAT DO THEY DO? WHAT HAPPENS WHEN A CONSULTANT IS ENGAGED? HOW TO HANDLE FINDINGS & RECOMMENDATIONS

Some companies refer to their internal compliance officer as a compliance consultant; an external compliance consultant has similar characteristics.

Aside from having the right credentials, expertise, and experience, the compliance officer's overall responsibility is to make sure that the organization complies with all laws and regulations that govern its business. To assure that employees are aware of an organization's expectations in terms of the Code of Conduct, education and training are a must. A company should want their employees to, "Say something whenever they see something." The compliance officer/professional plays an essential part in many ways, e.g. they assist leadership to understand why it relates to the tone of how the organization embraces compliance and integrity and its impact on the culture. The overall goal of any Compliance program should be to eliminate risk and maximize compliance. If risks can't be eliminated, then at least minimize them. They do that with the cooperation of everyone in the organization.

It is imperative for leadership to be at the forefront of the Compliance program by being the "bridge" that connects and encourages positive relationships between the Compliance Department and all staff. The first thing I do when I am engaged as a consultant is to ask senior leadership this question: "How committed are you to compliance?" Their response lets me know if I would have their full support and insight into the corporate culture. When developing and implementing a Compliance program, a cultural change is bound to happen. These changes may result in resistance from some employees as they are required to change how they do some things or EVERYTHING.

Once I have the leadership's support, I ask them to let all appropriate staff know that the compliance officer or compliance consultant, while on engagement, should be granted access to whatever information is requested. The compliance consultant can ask for anything relevant to the project and they should receive full cooperation. If they request personnel records, corporate reports or financial documents they should be able to have access. The compliance consultant should be trusted to manage and maintain confidential information.

When a company hires a compliance officer, they should expect the new person to partner with leadership including the president, CEO, senior vice president, and chief financial officer to either build or enhance the ethical culture. The company's leadership MUST have a communication plan that advises all employees: "We hired a compliance officer whose responsibilities include… our main objective is to assure our organization is in compliance with all laws and requirements. Our new compliance officer is going to help us accomplish this. As a result, there may be changes to the way we do business and we are excited about this."

When the compliance officer or consultant's role is effectively communicated, and employees see management's support, they are inclined to be welcoming instead of resistant. There is a connection between a compliance officer and consultant with ROI. Either position should increase the company's ROI.

The organization's ROI can happen quicker when everyone is honest about the company's past and present issues/problems. Being transparent about everything allows the compliance officer or consultant to develop a strategic plan to help address the problems.

My message to the leadership team is, "Set the tone." From the onset, I inquire by asking them: "How committed are you?" The correct response should be: "We are 100% committed, and that's why we have you here."

My next question is, "Do you understand what is going to happen as a result of you engaging me?" This is a HUGE undertaking. I tell them not to think or say, "Okay, once the contract/engagement is completed, we have a Compliance program and plan. Thank you; we are all set, now the consultant can go away." It is important for me to make them aware that compliance is a journey. You will never be 100% perfect/compliant, but you sure can get close. Building a Compliance program that works depends on hiring the right people and putting a significant budget behind it.

My experience working with non-profit organizations is that some struggle with allocating the appropriate funding for training, staffing, and technology to name a few. The leadership will cut the Compliance program budget if they must cut funding because they believe compliance costs and there may not be an immediate ROI. Why? Because we are talking about resources including staff. It costs money to have enough staff on the compliance team that can help with all initiatives, especially if an organization is in multiple states and/or has an international presence. A decent budget is needed because it takes more than one person to develop, implement, monitor, and audit a compliance program.

The organization will have an advocate in the compliance officer or consultant as they develop or enhance their program. The compliance professionals can identify missing requirements the organization didn't know needed to be in place.

A compliance officer or consultant is not a magician; they can't make things appear or go away. They are not enforcers which is a stereotype many people get wrong. Sometimes compliance officers unjustly get a bad reputation. When employees see their co-workers being demoted or terminated as the result of a compliance audit, they attribute the action to the compliance officer. Some become fearful of compliance officers when they shouldn't be; we are all on the same team or should be.

As a company strives to assure it complies with all the laws and regulations of their industry, it must help all employees know they are essential. The bottom line is the compliance officer is just trying to make sure that the right things happen. To reiterate, compliance officers are not magicians and they are not the enforcer of what needs to be implemented. I look at their role as one more of monitoring; it is leadership's responsibility to enforce the organization's commitment to compliance. Compliance officers are there to make sure the company is adhering to its compliance plan. They conduct, or work with those who conduct risk assessments of the company's operations.

How do you know what to fix if you don't know what's broken? I HIGHLY recommend doing risk assessments at least once annually. Depending on the problems that emanate as the result of audits or other situations, it may be necessary to conduct the risk assessment more often. When a plan is established that will mitigate risks, a compliance officer should ask the appropriate leadership: "Who on your staff is assigned to the responsibility of fixing the problem(s)?" Leadership in the operational area where the problems exist should be enforcing the risk assessment plan. Whatever plan or remedies developed should be implemented.

WHEN IS THE RIGHT TIME TO BRING IN A CONSULTANT?

This section discusses various types of organizations that can engage a compliance consultant when there is a need. It is impossible, because the list is too long, to indicate all business types. However, this section gives a clear picture of who may need a compliance consultant and when they are recommended.

START-UPS

Leadership at start-up companies don't know what they don't know as it relates to compliance because they may have never heard of a compliance officer or compliance program. When is the right time to engage a consultant?

Maybe the leadership knows nothing about compliance programs or the need for developing and implementing one. If the new business receives government funding, somewhere in the contract and documentation, the word compliance was probably mentioned. The best thing a start-up can do from the beginning is to hire a compliance officer or engage an experienced compliance consultant to help them identify and understand what is needed to be compliant in their industry. Start-ups should look for someone with knowledge and experience on laws and regulations that govern their business.

When there are state requirements, is the start-up meeting those requirements? If the start-up is setup as a corporation, they may need to be aware of different requirements that do not apply to a start-up operating as a sole proprietor, and are they filing those requirements as mandated by state laws? Regulatory and legal requirements can be overwhelming for most people. Therefore, start-ups without prior knowledge and experience can benefit from speaking with an experienced attorney and a compliance consultant. Both professionals can attest to the value of a compliance program. Partnering with a consultant beforehand is going to help start-ups be more successful, avoid pitfalls, unnecessary problems, and some of the growing pains many start-ups encounter.

The last thing you want to do when setting up your company is to do everything right and then forget to take care of a critical filing or forget to review key documentation before billing the insurance company. Technology is expanding constantly and there are tools that will help make sure that the company stays on track. A compliance consultant can help a start-up develop a strategic plan for establishing an effective Compliance program and plan.

LARGE CORPORATIONS OR COMPANIES EXPANDING NATIONALLY OR INTERNATIONALLY

You would be surprised by the number of companies without a formal Compliance program in place, which is a major liability. There are both legal and regulatory requirements for companies looking to operate in multiple states and/or countries.

As with start-ups, the best time for expanding companies to hire a consultant is BEFORE they start the expansion process, whether nationally, or internationally. A compliance consultant can identify key requirements that might discourage a company from expanding to a city, state, or country. Some companies started making costly changes and plans only to find out too late that they were not able to comply with requirements to operate in the new territory. I recommend EVERY organization have a compliance officer, or someone responsible in the role of carrying out the responsibilities of a compliance officer, such as a compliance consultant and a compliance program.

You might be wondering, what things, a consultant can do to help when an organization is looking to expand geographically. Well, if the company wants to expand to other states or even internationally, it is in their best interest to understand the new state's or country's requirements regarding business. Every state and country have their own nuances, different regulatory requirements and laws; it is imperative for a company to engage a good attorney if they don't have one and a consultant able to exercise due diligence on their behalf. An attorney can make sure the organization is structured correctly and that its designation status is appropriate.

Also, a consultant can help with establishing a plan for expansion and monitoring compliance. Does the company have the appropriate license(s) to conduct business in the new state(s)? What about certifications; does the company have ALL the required certifications and licenses? Is it enough to be getting them or should they first be approved?

The same considerations are relevant when an organization plans to expand internationally. Here, the organization would have to comply with various rules and regulations because they would have both domestic and foreign corporation status. For example, when a company is in New York and opens an office in Germany, the company in New York would receive domestic status while the company in Germany would receive foreign status.

Are there any international industry-specific councils or forums the organization can join to get familiar with a new country and its rules? Many companies may not think about or consider contacting an international council or trade association or even know they might be available.

Each country is different and the best advice I give organizations when looking to expand internationally is research. A lot of this information, thanks to technology, can be looked up online. However, the VERY first thing I recommend is to hire an attorney who is well versed and licensed to practice law in the country where they are looking to expand. The selected attorney should know the industry and know it well.

My experience working with organizations doing business in multiple states and in several countries, taught me the importance of due diligence. Each state's laws may vary per state. The same can be true in other countries; there are city requirements, country requirements and more than likely that may differ per region. Again, it is wise to engage a compliance consultant experienced working on an international level, to work with the law firm hired to exercise the required and strongly advised, due diligence.

Second on the must-do list is to hire an accounting firm. Why? Simply because the company will be dealing with different tax laws. Companies looking to expand to other countries need someone or an accounting firm that understands international tax laws, local tax requirements, tax filings, and all the other tax-related concerns that come with doing business in other countries. I used to work for a company with offices in other countries; our international employees were taxed differently from our USA-based employees.

A COMPANY WITHOUT A COMPLIANCE PROGRAM IN PLACE

Some companies are not aware they should or are required to have a Compliance program due to the nature of the work, services or products they provide. In this instance, I recommend a company brings in a consultant as soon as yesterday. Why? I probably sound redundant saying this; however, it demonstrates how strongly I feel, because the consultant can help build a compliance program, and sometimes help with or guide the implementation process.

Maybe the company has no Code of Conduct, however, they may have a policy on professionalism, which is included in a Code of Conduct. It would help the company to get a compliance officer. That person should know the laws, regulations, and requirements relevant to their business. Until a compliance officer is on board, it would be prudent to engage a consultant; this person can serve as the interim compliance officer until the company is prepared to create and fill the full-time position.

Education is crucial. How are employees supposed to conduct themselves in the workplace? How and when are they supposed to report allegations of misconduct? We have a saying in the industry: "When you see something, say something." But who are they supposed to tell? Who do you want them to report it to? How are they supposed to report it? What happens with retaliation? Guess what? It's real, it happens. Do you have a zero tolerance for retaliation policy and are your employees aware of it? Do you have an open-door policy? What do you do when you are a company Senior VP or manager and allegations of fraud, abuse, or sexual harassment surfaces throughout the organization due to employees reporting? How are you gauging improvement? Do you even care? These are some of the topics I cover when I consult with organizations to educate their employees and upper management. To prepare for the training, I collect as much information as possible about the organization to ensure it aligns with the company's goals, principles, mission, vision, and values.

When is the perfect time to answer these questions? The executive leadership team should be able to address questions during the initial meetings.

Why? A compliance officer and consultant can be instrumental in helping with due diligence, e.g. conducting research, and regulatory requirements. The companies with legal counsel who collaborate with the compliance department have a better chance for an effective compliance program.

The partnership between counsel and compliance enables the company to have a robust Compliance program and a strong-fearing ethical culture. This initiative reinforces the company's expectations by communicating the "rules" via the Code of Conduct. The code of conduct provides rules and guidelines. I am a firm believer if you tell people the rules, they can play the game. The last thing companies should do is wait until the code of conduct is established to begin creating rules because employees would have learned certain behaviors and formed bad habits. Not effectively and timely communicating the "rules" make it harder to change or modify later.

Employees rarely appreciate a new compliance officer, or compliance professional, coming on board and telling everyone:

"Oh, you guys have been doing this all wrong." Or saying: "You should have done that this way." Some employees become complacent with the way things are or the way they have been doing things. This group of employees creates opposition and it would have been easier to set the rules initially such as during new employee orientation (NEO), instead of changing the rules in the middle of the game.

In the structure of traditional organizations, information flows from the top down; many call it the Trickle-down Theory. When change is inevitable, it is wise to include employees, who usually oppose everything on committees that address problems. These employees will more than likely become your ally. Allowing employees to feel included in the change process is a recipe or formula for success.

What if you are starting a small business and you will be the first employee, should you even bother consulting with a compliance officer or consultant?

The short answer is a resounding: ABSOLUTELY. You may be a one-person operation; I briefly spoke about this under the section: who should have a compliance program. My response was, "ALL organizations." I don't care if you have one employee or ten million; every industry has laws and regulations and if you are conducting business, the company must comply with them. If you are a solopreneur, there is a term called self-compliance. What are you telling your clients? I had a client who owns a candy and baking company; she does it all herself. There are regulations in the state where she resides, and she must comply to the regulations that apply to her business involving the health department. When I consulted with her, I advised her to remember two things. One, she needed to be aware of laws and regulations in every state her company operated. Since she started her business, she and her family moved from New Hampshire to Oklahoma and now they live in North Carolina. Each state has specific regulations and every time they moved, I advised her to get acquainted with all requirements pertaining to her baking and candy enterprise. She avoided fines and unnecessary issues by listening to my advice.

In my role as a consultant, I had her looking into both federal and state requirements, tax laws and codes of conduct for bakers. What was she committing to her clients? What was her policy about client inquiries? If she advertised responses would be made within 24-hours, did that actually happen? What about the return policy, and the quality of her baked goods? What claims did she make? "I bake goods and make candy with the highest-grade quality. My chocolate chip cookies have the richest quality and flavor. The chocolate chips I use blow Nestlé's out of the water?" I asked her: "Who says that they are better than Nestlé's? You are making these statements so how do you quantify and qualify them?" I made the same recommendations to a friend who also is a baker and ships her product around the United States. I say this to solopreneurs: "You still need to have a code of conduct, even though you are the only person in the company. You still need to know the laws and regulations that govern your business." The clients got it, they made changes by putting policies in place that addressed ALL my questions and concerns.

Besides a compliance plan, small businesses should have a quality and customer service plan. They should have information on their website that addresses their commitment to ethics, quality customer service, and all regulatory requirements. What is their pledge? What is their commitment as a business owner? What do they say to their customers regarding quality and integrity? After 20-years of experience, I believe it doesn't matter if you are a solopreneur, you still need a compliance program. It may be different and look different from the Compliance program of a company with fifty, two thousand or five hundred thousand employees; a program can still be beneficial.

A common question I am often asked is "I'm a solopreneur, are there places I can go to find a compliance officer or consultant that works with businesses of my size?" Business owners can Google compliance consultants in their area, ask other small business owners for a referral/recommendation or contact a trade association. Referrals and/or word of mouth might be the best way to find a qualified compliance consultant. I enjoy working with small businesses; there is something exciting about helping to develop and implement a compliance program. *Subscribing to risk and compliance magazines would be a great place to look too.

Remember to do industry-specific searches as the rules and regulations vary by industry even within the United States. For example, the compliance and ethics for mortgages is specific to the mortgage industry, the banking industry has their own set of laws and regulations. *See at the end of the book an example of a resource for business owners in the restaurant business.

Why did I share all those resources with you? Because businesses, large and small have no excuse when it comes to knowing their industry's compliance requirements.

There are many listservs that are specific to industry, specialty, etc. and too many to list here!

A COMPANY WITH A COMPLIANCE PROGRAM IN PLACE

Why should they bring in a consultant? They already have a program in place. Yes, that might be true, but do they have everything they are supposed to have in place? What about persistent disciplinary issues due to lack of compliance? Do they have different options available for employees to report? Is the company required to pay fines and penalties due to compliance issues? Do they know how to handle delicate situations and engage with the right department, leadership, or employee?

Are they set up to discover, identify, and remedy gray areas and/or blind spots? If you read ALL those questions and felt uneasy about one of them, then it is NOT too early to call in a consultant. Every organization needs experienced external eyes at some point, on their Compliance program because those monitoring it can be too close and might miss some yellow, orange and even blatantly bright red flags.

Another valid reason is to keep transparency. A compliance officer might say: "We have the best Compliance program because we are doing everything right. Compliance is my department and my responsibility." But is that true? Many things might be running smoothly while others could benefit from having an external third party perform an audit of the entire program. There is nothing to lose; companies can avoid aggravation and save lots of money in the long run.

Engage an external consultant to assess various aspects of a company's business to determine if any gaps exist. Are there any vulnerabilities? Did we do everything we were supposed to do? Are there things we are doing well but can find easier ways to do them? Are there other benefits, enhancements, and improvements that can be made? It's always good to have an extra set of eyes to look at your program and assess what you have in place and to make sure everything is as it should be.

When I was the VP of Corporate Compliance for an international company, I suggested our Compliance program be audited by a third party. I wanted us to be doing things correctly. Even then I knew audits and consultants were not to be feared or alienated but leverage for the wellbeing of the program and the company as a whole.

One of my former employers was international and had locations in multiple states. I delegated responsibilities to other people including my staff who would spend time in the field conducting audits and providing training. The environment was fast-paced; there was always something happening/going on. We tracked the regulatory agencies that would come. Due to the industry and the number of programs we had, the company routinely had regulatory agencies on site conducting audits. This being the case, I had the compliance department provide a detailed report on the number of regulatory agency visits to management, the Compliance Committee and the Board of directors on a quarterly basis.

The organization was always being audited, reviewed or assessed so it behooved us to endeavor to stay on top of things. This entailed making sure all documentation was present and accurate; billing was being done correctly, and they were reporting as required. When there were gaps in reporting, it was important to know how to rectify the problem. There was always something happening at the organization and I wanted to always be in a pro-active mode instead of a reactive one.

Want to know a not-so-well-kept secret? When the government shows up, they can stay at a company or business as long as they want and return as often as they want. They can say something like: "We are just here to…we just want to make sure you are taking care of our beneficiaries; we noticed…its's been report-ed…." A company or organization who continually has issues like an overpayment, allegations of fraud, documentation errors and significant findings during external audits can trigger a visit from a regulatory agency.

A COMPANY GOING THROUGH A MERGER OR ACQUISITION

A company going through a merger or acquisition would want to have a compliance program. Hopefully, they have a compliance officer in place. Mergers and acquisitions require a company to exercise their due diligence. The company doing the acquiring may have their own compliance program; however, it is critical to re-view the other company's compliance systems and protocols. What do they have in place? If they are not doing anything or don't have an "active" compliance program, then that means the company ac-quiring has to start from scratch. Essentially the companies could be merging systems, protocols, and staff. In order for the process to be successful, engaging an experienced attorney and compliance consultant can mitigate disruption and costly mistakes.

When considering a merger or acquisition, contemplate these questions: Are they or were they ever in trouble with any regulatory bodies or state government? Did they have to pay fines? Did they have any penalties? Are they under review? Are they on the list excluding them from government contracts? Are they forbidden from receiving government funding? Are there sanctions against them? Are they under a Compliance and Integrity Agreement (CIA) with the government? If yes, that means that for the next three to five years the organization must submit a report to the government addressing designated information and have to do a plan continuously.

A company is placed under a CIA when they have done something naughty. In all fairness, a company's bad behavior may not have been intentional.

The company doing the acquiring or going through merger should carefully review the results of the due diligence. If the other company has a situation that is or can be too problematic or become a major liability, then it may be wise to back out of the proposed deal. Legal counsel could guide the process from beginning to end.

A COMPANY THAT IS UNDER PERSISTENT DISCIPLINARY ISSUES DUE TO LACK OF COMPLIANCE

Companies with continuous problems due to lack of compliance are the perfect example of organizations that would GREATLY benefit from having a consultant come in to help discover what is causing the problems, what policies are not working or not being enforced, or if key staff are responsible for the ongoing issues.

I had that experience while consulting with an organization. When I began my review, I realized the company had no Compliance program and their employees never received training on policies and procedures. They were just creating documents and saying: "Woohoo, we have a compliance program." Nobody was auditing, nobody was educating, nobody was training. Meanwhile, they were incorrectly submitting claims to the funder for several years. The issue was discovered during an external audit and everything went downhill from there. They had promoted a person into the compliance officer position. The problem was the person was inexperienced. Even in working and trying to fix things, the compliance officer, still not knowing what to do and not knowing where to get help, thought they were doing the right thing. Their actions made things worse.

I call it the ripple effect because if you don't know what you are doing over here, you are not going to know what to do over there. The company was in multiple states and had locations within each state and every operational area had issues because most of the senior leadership had the same management team responsible for all the operations. They were running beyond capacity with no training, resources or support.

The compliance officer never picked up on the issues because they just didn't know what they did not know. The main issue was a lack of compliance; they created what was thought to be a great program and plan, but it turned out to be a fiasco. The plan lacked communication, training, reporting protocols, monitoring, disciplinary measures, and an auditing system wasn't in place to ensure they were being compliant within their industry.

They have made significant improvements in some areas but still have a way to go until all their operations have been assessed. The company could have supported the compliance officer by sending her to conferences for educational purposes, allowed her to join trade associations, and professional organizations. They could have engaged a consultant much sooner.

The first mistake this company made, and unfortunately, many non-profit organizations make this mistake, was believing that hiring an experienced compliance professional or consultant is an expensive cost they can't bear. Their first question is: "What is our ROI going to be if we do this?" It just baffles me when they don't understand the importance or the value of having a Compliance program in place.

Some companies do the following by thinking, "Okay, the government says we have to hire a compliance officer because we are getting money from the government. Let's just name person X as our compliance officer." It is not THAT simple because a compliance officer/professional requires a particular skill set. The person appointed to that position must be able to communicate with people on all levels, both inside and outside of the organization.

The person should have analytical skills as they are constantly analyzing things; something as simple as: "Was that infraction or misconduct committed intentionally or do they need additional training?" Compliance officers have many skills; they must understand how to read and interpret laws and regulations, as well as be able to multitask.

Compliance professionals must be able to deal with problematic staff and have a reputation of being integral because they handle more confidential matters and problematic situations than any other persons in leadership. There is so much information they are regularly privy to and the ability to keep information confidential is key. In essence, they know where the bodies are buried in the organization.

For compliance officers to succeed, the chain of command and reporting protocol are relevant. Having the right leadership in place and effective communication helps to facilitate the process. The compliance officer is generally a member of the management team. Depending on a company's structure, they may report directly to the president, CEO, CFO, or a senior VP (if they are not a senior VP themselves). Why is this necessary? It is necessary because the position requires a person to be in authority and have high-level oversight.

Again, being a compliance officer/compliance professional and consultant requires a skillset; naming or appointing one who lacks the right skills and background is never the right thing to do. The ideal candidate must understand your business and the laws of your business. They might not know everything; however, they should have the acumen and willingness to learn. I had to learn; I didn't come into the compliance arena knowing everything. I networked, joined professional trade associations, and subscribed to listservs to find out the current climate, e.g. cutting-edge technology, current regulatory requirements, and the latest and the greatest in my industry.

COMPANIES FACING FINES AND PENALTIES
DUE TO COMPLIANCE ISSUES

Every organization should have access to legal counsel. The best course of action if a company must pay fines and penalties is to work with their attorney to help resolve those issues. Why is that? By doing so everything discussed with the attorney may be done under attorney-client privilege. After those issues are resolved, a compliance consultant can be engaged to help the company strategize, develop and implement policies, systems, training, and protocols. For the strategy to be effective, the compliance officer should step out, and let the consultant step in so they can identify the gaps. Moreover, they can collaborate with leadership, including the compliance officer to develop a plan that will prevent the company from making the same mistakes in the future.

A very good friend, who also works in the Compliance field, is the VP of Compliance for an entity classified as a healthcare provider. She also has her own consulting business, where she is highly skilled in helping companies with their Corporate Integrity Agreements (CIA). Integrity agreements are required* when an organization is sanctioned by the government, because either they are in trouble or did something wrong.

As defined by the Office of Inspector General, a **Corporate Integrity Agreement (CIA)** is:

"a document that outlines the obligations to which an entity agrees as part of a civil settlement. An entity agrees to the CIA obligations in exchange for the Office of Inspector General's (OIG) agreement that it will not seek to exclude the entity from participation in Medicare, Medicaid, or other Federal

health care programs. CIAs have common elements, but each one is tailored to address the specific facts of the case and may incorporate elements of a pre-existing compliance program."

An integrity agreement (IA) is a document that outlines the obligations to which an individual practitioner, small group practice, or small provider agree as part of a civil settlement.

The companies under a CIA are listed on the OIG's website; and it is public information. The companies must do routine reporting to the government to demonstrate they have or are making recommended changes.

My friend the VP works with organizations who have been added to that list and are under a CIA. She assesses the identified problems, reviews all notices, and reports. She helps write her client's agreement, documents what they are committed to do, helps them create a project schedule, and their action plan. Last, she monitors the process to ensure they do what they say they will do. Due to the cause and length of a CIA, my friend sets up long-term engagements that cover the agreement from the beginning to the end. Often, her clients ask her to extend the contract after the agreement to include additional monitoring for six (6) months to one (1) year.

The BIG message of this section is: This is not the time to be skimpy, the moment you see fines, and penalties, get somebody in the door ASAP.

To reiterate, you may have a lawyer and a compliance officer who will be assisting you. It may be beneficial to hire a consultant highly skilled in the area(s) you are struggling with and can help prevent the issues from reoccurring. When considering a compliance consultant, don't just focus on someone with experience in the areas where you have the fines and penalties but also in operations, and anywhere else you may have vulnerabilities.

*For additional information go to the OIG and HHS (Health and Human Services) website (search for: Corporate Integrity Agreement).

WHAT TO DO WHEN A CONSULTANT IS BROUGHT IN?

We will look at the perspective of setting up a company's structure; establishing the mindset of the people to be interacting with the compliance firm or consultant directly preparing upper-management and communicating with the consultant about the company's culture. Knowing both the company's and consultant's expectations during an engagement should be established in the initial meetings. This could be as simple as providing the resources they need. For example, sending a message to appropriate staff advising them of their responsibility to cooperate with all requests and creating a work environment that meets the consultant's needs can facilitate the client-consultant relationship.

It is also a good idea to: provide a dedicated space with doors that lock (to safeguard sensitive information and documents), have a contact person or liaison assigned to the consultant, talk to employees about confidentiality, provide the consultant with a secure laptop, access to secure printing and access to files and pertinent documentation. The list is important, but a company also should advise their employees how they should act around the consultant, how to deal with impropriety, in giving the consultant things they are not free to provide, or buying gifts, lunches or perks.

One of the most important initiatives is communicating with key personnel so all employees know that a consultant will be on site. Also, employees should be respectful, professional and mindful of the conversations within earshot of a consultant and other visitors, i.e. government auditors. Then, guidelines about transparency should be given to those who will be working with the consultant. Whatever the consultant requests should be provided and as quickly as possible. Upper management must encourage their staff to answer all questions during the interview process. As a consultant, I usually start interviewing key staff on the first day of the engagement. Part of the reason for the interview is to discover workflows, processes, systems, and where information lives.

Let's say a company may have committed some type of fraudulent act or they can't trace documentation for billable services. They may have to pay money back to the government or whatever funder is involved. I would conduct interviews to determine who, what, and where the breakdown in the process occurred. It's important for the people I would speaking with to be forthcoming with information. The consultant is there to help, not to hurt. They are there to find solutions to problems that will ultimately improve things. I can't fix something if I don't know where it's broken; that is why transparency is key. Before I begin the engagement, I give my contact person a list of what I need and the people I may need to interview. Having this set up before I come in saves time. I subscribe to the cliché "time is money." Therefore, I don't have time to waste.

Sometimes employees get nervous or scared when a consultant is hired because they know their department's vulnerabilities will surface and they are thinking: "Oh my God, she is going to find out." They try to fix things. Whatever you do, do not alter; this is not the time to change and/or create documentation and records. You will be exposed because a good consultant will figure it out. Why do I say that? Because I've seen employees create documents that did not previously exist to avoid getting in trouble with a consultant and auditor. It is not the consultant or auditor they should be concerned about as much as the leadership. I have and continue to work with leadership who want their organization to be in compliance; they want to get it right. It becomes the reason they consult with me.

Understand that not all cases of fraud are intentional; sometimes people don't know what they don't know. Employees generally continue doing things that were wrong because of the way they were trained. Whoever set up the practice or was previously responsible for the process, often is the same person that trains or hires the next person. The incorrect practice perpetuates and the wrong way of doing things continues. In these cases, the fraud, although it is still fraud, would be considered unintentional. A consultant or compliance officer can help with establishing a matter of discovering where the problems are and how to fix them. When employees do not know what they are doing is wrong, it doesn't absolve them of the consequences. As the government or funder may say, "When you signed up to be a provider of services or to take on certain contracts, and you are receiving money, you will know the guidelines." Again, not knowing doesn't absolve an organization and its leadership from misconduct because of their ignorance of the requirements.

You might be wondering, so Dr. Robyn, what do companies do to create an ideal environment for a consultant? For starters, the initial contact is with the president, CEO or one of the senior VPs. During our preliminary conversation, I tell them what is needed and why. A communication plan is part of the process; I encourage them to send one to their key stakeholders and the rest of the organization. I have templates that can be used that provide the language for an announcement that can be well understood and received by all employees.

I promote transparency and the organization's commitment to it must come from the very top; otherwise, the staff may push back and not follow the rules. When management doesn't support the compliance officer or consultant's initiative, getting full cooperation is like pulling teeth. I usually have a follow-up conversation with the senior leadership that brought me on board. I say something like: "I don't know what's going on around here. I had a conversation with x, y, and z thinking they understood they needed to give me what I requested but they did not. I can't help you if I don't have the documentation, can you please remind them to give me what I require?" It never ceases to amaze me how *fast* staff cooperates after they receive a call from upper management.

Because every engagement is different, the communication disseminated throughout an organization is tailor-made for that organization and that engagement. For example, sometimes I'm there to conduct an audit. Other times, I'm there to do an investigation before they hire me for a longer and more in-depth engagement. It just depends on the engagement and the company's needs at the moment. For example, when it's a financial or billing audit where an organization is being accused of fraud, such as submitting false claims to the government, that's one type of communication. If I'm there to investigate allegations of fraud, waste, abuse or gross misconduct, then that's a different communication.

I recommend organizations consider their community because that will help determine how they should communicate with them. If the company is run like a tight-knit community, sending a cold or indifferent memo won't be well-received by the staff. Additionally, the organization should be consistent in the way they communicate with employees. If leadership prefers departmental meetings, then key information should be shared in that form. If leadership chooses a town hall-style meeting, then they should use that approach. My experience has taught me to always be mindful how employees are accustomed to being notified of changes or updates.

It is necessary to have someone appointed to be the "go to person" or designated contact for the consultant. When appropriate, let people know who the appointed person is. Why? The designated contact person can serve as the key internal person for tracking and documenting all requests. The contact person should develop a list of every document requested.

While consulting, I advise an organization of the following: when an auditor, contractor, or consultant requests something, e.g., books or records, whatever is being asked of you, document everything. Document what was requested, who requested it, and the date and time of the request. If records are distributed, document when they were given and returned. Valuable records could be lost or misplaced, or a consultant might walk out the door with some of your original documentation. The organization should know who gave it, when they gave it, and when and if it was returned.

Depending on the engagement, I might request training records, employee personnel files, time cards (time sheets), electronic records, and work schedules. When available, videos and other documentation that can relate to the audit is also requested.

When I am engaged to investigate, I may need to visit an employee's workspace. I have investigated allegations made by an employee regarding something they heard, something they saw on a computer screen, or something they watched an employee do. Visiting and assessing the workspace can provide pertinent information; depending on the setup, the allegation(s) might have no basis. For example, if the accused employee's back is up against a wall in their workspace and their computer screen is facing them then somebody walking by could not see anything. A person can't come behind them; so, my question to the reporting person might be: "How were you able to see their screen?"

Consultants need a dedicated office or workspace while at a client's work site. It is recommended to provide a workspace with a door that locks. Generally, I prefer the office or workspace to be away from other consultants who might be working on-site for a different purpose and independent of my engagement/contractual arrangement, and an organization's employee population. I request a workspace/office be, if possible, away from employee traffic. Sometimes employees like to come by and talk about things with nothing to do with my engagement. That's not always a good thing. It is good when the information is relevant and related to my visit. Depending on what additional information is shared, I will report it to the appropriate person. The information can open up another "can of worms." It is possible the information might relate to the current situation and may be helpful.

WHAT DOES A CONSULTANT NEED IN THE OFFICE OR WORKING SPACE?

Most of the companies that engage me require that I use a company laptop provided by them that enables me to connect to their secure network. A telephone that can page key employees or have conference calls can be helpful. I use my work cell phone while I am on assignment and many consultants do that as well.

When a company does not have an extra office or workspace, they might place me in their boardroom or a regular conference room. These would work if there are no interruptions and the doors to the space lock. I must be able to lock the door because nine out of ten times some if not all of the documents I have been given access to contain confidential information, and as such must be protected. My laptop is encrypted so I don't worry about causing privacy or security breaches.

Often, an organization will give me access to their facilities by providing a fob and/or badge. My preference is to receive access daily and return the item by the end of each day upon my departure. It is simple; I sign in, they give me a key fob and/or the badge, at the end of the day I return it.

Why is that you may ask? I recommend organizations to always monitor who has access to their building at all times. Also, in the event of a natural disaster, safety issues, or health scare, the organization would be able to identify, and report all necessary information to the appropriate authorities. I know that a key fob and security badge can track a person's entry and exit from a building. Keeping those items until the engagement ends can be more convenient for some; however, I prefer otherwise. I return everything at the end of the day including files, documents, etc., and if I need those same files the next day, I'll request them. Sometimes, the site contact leaves files in the workroom space. I recommend all records be locked up. If they leave them in the room, I advise them to make sure they are double locked, meaning the files should be secured in a locked filing cabinet inside of the locked room/workspace. I also make sure that the contact person signs off; that there's a record indicating all files have been returned. I don't want to be accused of taking original files or believed that I have them.

How can this be helpful to you? You might be reading this book and consider hiring a consultant; these "small" things may not have crossed your mind. Perhaps you weren't aware why double locking files and locking the office or workspace is a great protocol to have in place for consultants. This initiative should be required for other departments within your organization when employees need access to certain books and records. Consider this: some consultants prefer unlimited access from the time they are given documents, often this can include weeks, NOT me. Another reason I prefer daily access is that I may become ill and can't make it into the site. If I have records in my possession and am gone for any length of time, you don't have immediate access to your records. This could cause chaos and major problems.

Let's talk about conducting interviews with staff and management, is it a good idea to have a witness, such as someone from Human Resources or a union representative, if applicable? The answer is yes, it is ALWAYS a good idea to have a witness or someone that can corroborate what was discussed during the interview, how the interview was conducted, and document the process just in case a complaint or concern is brought up later. When I conduct interviews, I prefer a person with me to transcribes the interview.

Once I had a situation where somebody was supposed to be with me when I had to conduct interviews; however, the person got sick and could not attend the interviews. I requested assistance from one of the administrative assistants at the company. If the situation or reason for the interview involved a serious allegation involving senior leadership, I do not use anyone inside of the organization. I would postpone the interview(s) until my assistant could join me. There are instances when the conversation/interview only entails discussing basic and/or non-confidential information. In these cases, I recruit another employee to serve as a witness; however, 99% of the time I have my assistant with me.

The interview transcription may become part of my findings and excerpts included in the final report depending on what is reported. Why? When people are interviewed, they may disclose confidential information or things that are critical. The information can be unrelated to the case; nevertheless, it can be important and may need investigation. It never fails, they always ask: "Is this going to be shared with leadership?" If they think their information will be shared, it may cause them not to report what they want me to know. At times, they feel they will be retaliated against. This is how I have answered that question, even when they pull back: "If it's going to impact the health, welfare, or well-being of someone or hurt the organization, then I'm obligated to share that information. I don't feel it is always necessary to say who said what. It's what was said that's important. So, if I have to report any information, I say what was communicated, but not who told me." This alleviates their concerns and fears of retaliation. The big distinction I make to employees is that I will always report information that may be detrimental to the organization or a particular person, but I will not reveal the identity of the person who shared it with me if possible.

SHOULD A COMPANY PROVIDE MEALS FOR CONSULTANTS?

Should a company provide meals for consultants? The short answer is no. Companies have different rules and practices. During one engagement, the staff stated they always order lunch for consultants. I always bring my own lunch/meals, water, and condiments. When a company orders lunch for staff or other consultants, I may accept a lunch; however, I offer money to pay for my lunch. It is not "illegal" to provide meals to a consultant if you are doing it for the right reason. I just prefer not to accept food or any other "gift."

WHAT THINGS OR BEHAVIOR'S SHOULD COMPANIES STAY AWAY FROM?

What things or behaviors should companies stay away from when bringing in a consultant? Previously, I discussed not offering bribes or anything that might be perceived as a bribe. I recommend companies disclose to their employees that a consultant is on the premises and where in the building they will be located. It is appropriate when you have a consultant in the office or government agency that employees are made aware. I have heard conversations I had no business hearing and I'm sure if the employees knew I was a consultant and why I was there, I wouldn't have heard those conversations.

It is unnecessary to tell all employees why a consultant is on site, only those who need to know should be informed. Some believe it depends on the engagement. If the purpose is to conduct an investigation, allegations of misconduct, sexual harassment, or abuse by someone in senior leadership, the "why" should not be disclosed. The reason the consultant is there may concern people and tempt certain employees to start tampering, altering documents, or recreating documentation. "Is she going to come to us next?" They might say to themselves. I don't want that to happen. Allowing employees to know a consultant is on the premises should be enough; however, those who need to know should know. Remind employees to be mindful of their conversations and to remain professional. Please don't make this type of announcement: "A consultant is going to be auditing the finance department." An announcement like that may cause some people to worry and prompt them to act inappropriately. Again, those who need to know, should be informed; sometimes that may involve an entire company.

I realize I am putting a lot of emphasis on this subject and for compelling reasons. I have had people try to hide "things", "fix" records after the fact, and recreate documents which appeared fraudulent. My response: "You have already billed for this service so why are you trying to alter it now? If it wasn't previously there, you should not include any missing documentation now." Not only the organization be committing fraud, they would have submitted claims that lacked the required documentation. I have seen people terminated for altering documents. Some compliance professionals believe the less information you share with employees regarding the purpose of an investigation or visit from an external agency will more than likely protect the integrity of the process.

I can tell stories for days. Let me tell you about the COO of an organization I had to investigate. The COO planted evidence in an employee's desk. The director of Human Resources walked by at the same time. The incident took place after hours; the HR director saw this COO at an employee's desk. During the investigation, I interviewed the man who had been falsely accused and was about to be terminated by the COO. The employee could not explain how the item got in his desk. The poor employee stated: "I never put it there. I don't know what happened, I was not at my desk and the item wasn't previously there." He categorically denied taking the item. When I conducted the interview, the COO was caught listening outside the door of the room where I met with the employee. The experience felt like the scene of a movie. Fortunately, the Human Resources Director was able to prove the COO had been at the accused employee's desk by documenting what he saw. At the end of the day, the COO was rightfully terminated. This man went to great lengths to set up an employee by planting evidence. Consequently, he had to be terminated. The issue started when another employee said a watch was stolen. To everyone's surprise, the entire time the watch had been taken by the company's COO.

The same COO had engaged his wife as a consultant to translate documents from English to Spanish. He paid her about triple the rate a translator would normally be paid. The COO had eight kids and his wife didn't work outside of the home. They had recently relocated for the job. Instead of sending the project out for bid, he hired his wife and paid her the exorbitant rate. The incredible thing is that the story does not end there. While I was conducting the audit and investigation, I realized that one day, the

COO took a company van and was using it for his personal use. Remember, I told you he had eight children. When I reviewed receipts, I noticed the COO had used his company credit card to fill up the van with gasoline; however, on the same day he had another gas receipt. The bottom line was he filled up his wife's car and the company van with gasoline using the company credit card. I asked myself: "How do you fill up a company car twice on the same day?" There was no logical response to indicate he traveled far enough to substantiate the need to service the company car twice in one day. As I went through his receipts and company credit card statements, I discovered he was doing the same thing with his personal vehicle. Unfortunately, he did a lot of unethical things.

There were several Code of conduct violations and all kinds of integrity issues with that case. No wonder the COO wanted to fire the employee and why he was listening outside the door while I was conducting the interview. He wanted to hear what people were saying about him. It's a good thing I use a white noise machine; those machines can make it difficult for others to eavesdrop on private conversations. I knew the walls in the building were paper thin, so I made sure a white noise machine was available. It is a practice I continue to adhere to, because you never know what people can hear or who is trying to hear. Companies should invest in white noise machines if their building has thin walls and confidentiality is a concern.

Are there any protocols for the person the company appoints as your contact person? Yes, and sometimes, it can be more than one person; it might be a team of three. As we move through the different phases of the engagement the number may change. For example, if I need somebody in finance to tell me how things are billed or their protocol, then the contact would be a key person from the finance department. Also, it could be someone in operations who knows the process, certain protocols, and flow. I may request to have a team of contacts for different phases of an engagement. It is important for the contact person to knows the process and the department being audited. The contact person could be an expert or the one responsible for managing a department or leading a team. It's usually someone high up in the chain who knows what's going on, is responsible for their department and understands how things are done. I always like someone in IT (Information Technology) available so I can have access to any internal system necessary to complete an engagement. Having a go-to person in IT makes my job easier and it expedites the process.

The consultant does not report to the appointed contact person(s). The contact(s) is not owed or entitled to any updates or briefings about an audit or investigation.

The contact person is there for the consultant's benefit and they may not be entitled to have any of the findings. When I am the consultant, my findings are submitted to whoever engaged me. Generally, I am engaged by the president of an organization, leadership team or the client's attorney.

I think it is good business practice to advise the contact person(s) how I operate, unless there is an emergency, I don't discuss findings until the assessment or audit is completed. Also, I don't provide briefings as I go through the process; the only person that gets briefed is generally the person that engaged me. If the CEO brought me in, they ask me for the status or for a brief update. "Where are you with this?" or "I'll wait until you are done." I have done this long enough to know when management needs to be updated or when I need to make a call and say things like: "This is what I found out today. I think you need to know this right away. It's worse than what you thought. I looked at these records and I can't find this money. I can't reconcile the books. This is what's on the line. You thought it was 2.2 million, well it might be more like 5.2 million instead."

Keeping the lines of communication open is key, especially when performing a financial audit. Leadership wants to know what is or could affect the company and impact their bottom line. The updates need not be formal; a quick phone call may suffice. When I don't get them the first time, I leave a voicemail requesting: "Please return my call. I want to give you an update on the status of the audit." That usually gets my calls returned quickly.

HOW TO HANDLE FINDINGS & RECOMMENDATIONS

If you are new to compliance and/or are a new compliance professional, you might be curious about what happens after an audit evaluation or investigation is completed. Should you immediately meet with an attorney when trouble is suspected or when things are uncovered during the audit process that the company may not have known? In this section, various scenarios are presented with a discussion on how the findings and recommendations might be provided. The information shared in this section was drawn from years of experience working in the compliance industry, training, and education.

At the conclusion of an audit, assessment, or investigation, I provide my clients with a comprehensive report of findings and recommendations thanks to a tool I created. The tool is used every time I am engaged to complete an assessment of a Compliance program or an audit.

Let's start with an audit/assessment. I review what is present and what should be present according to the **United States Sentencing Commission's (USSC)** recommendation for an effective compliance program. If the organization has everything in place, then all is well. If they don't, then there will be findings. If they have part of the required elements, they will receive recommendations on where they can improve their program and processes. Although the USSC's elements for effective compliance was required for a particular group, the assessment tool can be modified to apply to any industry. The elements can be used in every industry as they lay the foundation for building a solid compliance program.

When an organization has no compliance program, they receive a report outlining the areas out of compliance and recommendation of what elements must be implemented based on importance.

Often, clients do not have a formal compliance program; however, they have certain elements. My process, using the tool, is basic. I evaluate what the client has in place and make recommendations that will enhance their partial procedures including policies needed to establish and implement a robust compliance program. Each client receives detailed feedback and recommendations, for their particular industry.

*For your convenience a copy of "The 7 Key Elements of a Compliance program" has been added to the end of this book.

A compliance program audit, what does that look like? What happens after the engagement is completed? Should the report be presented in person or should leadership receive a written report or both?

At the completion of an audit or assessment, I meet with a company's leadership (the CEO, or whoever engaged me). Once the team(s) or the selected group of employees are present, I present the findings. Depending on the nature of the engagement, I may conduct a presentation or briefing, providing recommendations. The client can ask questions. Sometimes, I am contracted with an organization's attorney. In these cases, my report is submitted to the attorney. Why? Because the audit may be conducted under attorney-client privilege. During this scenario, I brief the attorney who may want me to communicate without the client present or with the attorney and the leadership. Sometimes, an attorney will have me present the findings and recommendations to the client and provide them with a copy of my report. The attorney may recommend I continue to work with the client after the engagement. In situations like that then a new contract is initiated and signed.

What if the client requires an audit? Are there any differences if it's an audit? What if they already have a Compliance program in place and you are doing an audit of documentation, billing, etc., is the process is still the same? Yes, it is.

WHAT IS INCLUDED IN THE FINAL REPORT? IF YOU SUGGEST OR RECOMMEND THAT THINGS BE FIXED OR PUT IN PLACE, DO YOU PROVIDE A PROPOSAL FOR YOU TO DO IT?

The report includes my findings, recommendations, and implementation suggestions; the recommendations are prioritized in order of importance. Also, the recommendation might suggest the implementation be done in phases. For example, the first phase may recommend they hire staff. The next phase might consist of consolidating or expanding operations. I don't tell a client they should hire me to oversee the implementation process; that's for the client to decide. It is in their best interest to hire me to oversee the implementation because I would be very familiar with their operation and what needs to be completed. I have been working with one of my current clients for a while and the results from the first engagement led to a second engagement. It's been two years and I still work with this client because they keep bringing me back to assist with other initiatives, e.g. training, new employee orientation, and coaching.

HOW DID THE ORGANIZATION THAT HIRED YOU KNOW YOU COULD HELP THEM WITH IMPLEMENTATION?

They were referred by their attorney as most of my clients are. I was presented as an expert in their industry and in setting up programs like theirs. During the engagement, the client saw me clean up their processes, develop policies, protocols, new systems, and training programs. It is not unusual for my clients to ask me to come on full-time. Why you may ask? Aside from helping them to develop compliance and integrity programs, provide solid recommendations following comprehensive audits, develop new systems and protocols, I have succeeded in helping clients mitigate settlements with the government over fraud allegations, improper billing, or abuse. One client conducts business in multiple states. The client was accused of fraudulent activity. I was engaged to complete a comprehensive audit based on the government report and allegations. As I was doing the research, looking at the investigation report and auditing them, I could find no communication from the state informing my client of the changes to billing and documentation guidelines they cited them for not following.

The state offered that they changed the criteria for billing this type of service. Ultimately, I could find no communication including written, text, email, etc. that informed or advised my client of changes. The guidelines had not been updated on the state's website. I informed the client they were partially at fault, because when they signed up to be a provider of this service, they should have read the small print. The small print advised the client and all providers of their responsibilities, i.e., knowing the expectations. I strongly believe the state was also at fault because we were unable to locate any communication to my client explaining the changes. We could find no documentation that suggested the process had changed. If the billing process changed, where and how did they inform the client?

Then, I devised a strategy that would require the client to refund money; however, we could minimize the financial impact. Part of the strategy was for my client to take responsibility for the "unintentional" mistakes and errors. Also, "We are unable to locate any communication, notices, emails, or correspondence from you that advised the providers of any changes explaining what we should have done, when we should have done it, or why we should have done it."

The outcome? Both the attorney and the client were amenable to the strategy. Corporate counsel facilitated the discussion, drafted, and sent the correspondence to the funder under their signature. Ultimately, my client's attorney succeeded in negotiating a reasonable settlement with the funder. Then every time they have a concern, I am told the president says: "Let's engage Robyn."

Before these problems emanated, the client appointed someone to be their compliance officer. Unfortunately, the person did not understand how to be a compliance officer. So, the company had no Compliance program or a resemblance of a compliance program; there wasn't anything in place. They were out of compliance and I said: "You are getting money from the government. You are required, for this industry, to have a compliance officer. Here's the citation, here are the guidelines, and this is what you should be doing." I not only told them but showed them exactly why and how they were out of compliance.

The first finding and recommendation on my report was for them to hire a compliance officer. That was the top priority and to their credit, they went through trying to bring someone on board. Ultimately, they asked me if I wanted the job! I immediately said no. I'm an entrepreneur and love the diverse consulting work I get to do. The fact is, I knew why I was saying no; it was the idea of going back to the beginning. When starting up a new division, especially at that level, the corporate compliance officer does not work 9-5. Depending on the size of the organization, number of employees, lines of business, and location, the compliance officer can potentially work nine to nine, five days a week and a lot of weekends. Taking on a full-time position with this client would initially require 12-14-hour days, especially since this company has a presence in multiple states in the USA and in other countries.

I knew EXACTLY the work it would take to develop and implement their compliance program. Don't get me wrong, I love doing what I do, but I had no desire to do what I did 15-years ago in the corporate sector. Eventually, the company made an offer and hired someone for the position. I provided them with a job description; I wished they had asked me for advice about who to hire. Not all compliance officers are created equal and the client's industry has many requirements. On the plus side, I still get to consult with them as needed.

6

WHAT TYPES OF BUSINESSES/ ORGANIZATIONS NEED A COMPLIANCE PROGRAM?

Based on my years of experience, especially in the field, these types of businesses would GREATLY benefit from having a Compliance and Industry Program:

Human services, health care, government agencies, non-profits, for-profits, entrepreneurs, churches and faith-based organizations, and small businesses.

One client owns a restaurant and catering business. I help them maintain compliance with regulations and assure all industry and state-specific requirements are understood and implemented.

I look at EVERY aspect of their business: Where they cook, how they cook, what they use to cook, how often they cater, and what their industry requirements include. What about the pledges they make to their customers regarding the integrity of the products they use? Just because my client loves the products they use and say they are the best does not make it factual. I ask the client how are they able to quantify and qualify their statement? Have they surveyed their customers? Do they know what the competition uses? I review and monitor the words used in their marketing communications and website content. What's the commitment and pledge? My team and I include those elements as part of our assessment.

I would love to see my client recognized by a national trade organization/publication for having quality products or winning an award for their products. If and when that happens, I want to make sure all their claims and pledges can be supported with documentation and data.

Why am I so adamant about this and feel is essential to have all the T's crossed and the I's dotted? Most entrepreneurs believe and say they are the best, do the best, and give the best but unfortunately, those are just words. They must be able to quantify and qualify their statements. Their position becomes a matter of ethics and integrity. This holds true for every industry; every organization needs a compliance program, including entrepreneurs. What about self-compliance?

Microsoft and Oracle both have a robust compliance program. As the demand for accountability increases, different businesses are developing and implementing compliance programs. I think you get the message, yes? Every industry can benefit from having a Compliance program.

I am currently working with a client who had appointed a compliance officer prior to engaging with me. The person is no longer employed with the organization. They did not understand what being a compliance officer entailed. The organization had no policies or procedures in place. The newly appointed compliance officer researched online and grabbed templates off the internet. Unfortunately, the compliance officer did not assist with developing and/or providing various education, training, or protocols. The consequences? My client is paying back large sums of money to the government because there was no documentation to back up the work they performed.

If employees are not educated on the requirements, they may not know the expectations. My client did not comply with the laws and regulations of their industry. However, things have turned around due to the new compliance and integrity program. This is a long-term engagement because they are a large company; they are in many states and have international offices. The engagement is long-term because we are auditing one company and program at a time. The company has offices in multiple states, we consider federal, state and local regulations. We continue to review and update their compliance program. Identifying problems and coming up with recommendations, protocols, and systems to help solve the ongoing issues is a priority. I periodically remind the leadership that compliance is a journey and it takes time to reach the goals.

I tell my clients: "Just because your company has a compliance officer and a Compliance program it does not mean the work is done. You shouldn't implement policies, procedures, and systems, audit them one time and then move on. You will *always* have to stay on top of things. The Compliance program should be evolving, it should never stay stagnant. As laws and regulations change, so should your program. Some systems or protocols may no longer work as well as they used to and require updating."

Conducting ongoing education and training is a great way to ensure everyone knows of the regulations and following the protocols and processes put in place. Remember, employees learn in different ways. For example, some employees like to read and don't want to watch the online training option, so give them ways to consume the training and material. Finding ways that help employees understand and apply what they learn can be challenging and is an ongoing process. It's never going to be perfect and there is always room for improvement.

How did I know that it will make a difference to have different ways to learn and educate instead of having one uniform way for an entire organization? I had to discover why a client continued to have the same problems within their organization. I was determined to discover what was wrong. Training directors developed educational programs for various initiatives; they were not working because critical mistakes were being made.

People learn differently, especially when working with employees from diverse cultures and educational backgrounds. When employees are from countries outside of the USA, English is not their first language. It's beneficial to have the information translated into their native language. Some companies may require employees to speak English to work for them. Having all documents, materials, etc. translated might help them better understand the expectations. Another consideration is age. It is normal to have employees who have been with a company twenty-thirty years and be older. The employee pool also included millennials; they are all about technology which might not be the same for the veteran employees.

Another point to consider involves an employee's position in the organization. Depending on responsibilities, employees are busy, and they may not have 30-minutes to sit through a training because they have a heavy workload and deadlines to meet. Most executives and managers are in meetings *all* the time. A simple solution might be setting up a webinar or some other platform that allows staff to access training by logging in, starting and stopping as often as necessary, and giving them a reasonable timeframe to finish would make a HUGE difference for implementation and high completion rates. Some employees prefer a face to face encounter. When possible, a company should direct trainers to conduct in-person presentations; because employees could attend and ask questions.

Other employees prefer to listen to the training because they can multitask and keep working. Some employees prefer to watch PowerPoint presentations instead of listening. They like to watch and read the content while others may prefer a different combination.

Again, it is important for organizations who want to have successful educational and training programs to remember that employees are on different levels and learn in different ways. The information should be made accessible and available to meet the need of both the organization and its employees.

This revelation was eye-opening for me. Most people would agree the subject matter in the field of compliance can be full of legalese; many employees are turned off by it. Based on my years of experience, I have discovered one of the best ways to communicate compliance education, e.g. regulations and laws, is by telling stories. The challenge becomes presenting the content, so it enlightens people instead of boring them. It is all right and recommended to add humor when appropriate.

When I worked in corporate America, I created a formula for my staff to use whenever we created training. The training had to meet certain criteria before it was approved for dissemination, so employees could transfer the knowledge to their jobs.

The formula was: $E+E+E = E$. The training had to be enlightening, exciting and engaging for it to be educational. Effective compliance education is necessary for every organization. If employees are not properly being educated how are they going to know what they are supposed to do? How can they play the game if they don't know the rules? I admonish leadership of the following: "Help your employees. If you want them to play the game, you must tell them your rules. When the rules change, you have to tell them."

I am a researcher at heart and studied how compliance education and training could be more effective and impactful. My team and I considered various ways employees learn. Over time, we found offering multiple ways for them to learn yielded positive results. There were decreases in billing and documentation errors and increases in retention. A benefit of providing various learning platforms prevents employees from saying they didn't know, or they didn't understand because they are given options from receiving the information. Document the types of education and training offered, the number of times it was offered and when employees received the information.

A compliance officer, who is appointed to the position and has little or no experience may not know all the nuances of developing a robust compliance education and training program. It is possible they will cut corners; the newly appointed compliance officer doesn't know what they don't know. Unfortunately, they can be placed in a position outside of their comfort zone and expertise.

NON-PROFIT ORGANIZATIONS

Most non-profit organizations rely on in-kind donations from people or other organizations for sustainability; they might get money from the government. Consider an organization such as the Red Cross. Whenever someone makes a donation or a contribution they can indicate where they want the money to go. I recall what happened after the 9/11 attacks and other major fatalities. The outpouring of sympathy was tremendous. People sent donations and designated where they wanted their money to go. However, not all donations, according to media reports were allocated to the appropriate funds as indicated. News reports and other media outlets alleged the leadership in these organizations confiscated the money and did whatever they wanted to do with it. Other rumors suggested some executives stole people's donations and used it on themselves.

In some instances, it was proven the organization had no accountability or structure in place to trace what happened to all the donations. This is an example of why having thorough systems in place is crucial and why compliance and integrity programs are essential. For those who are unfamiliar with contributing to a non-profit, remember when people contribute money and designate to a specific cause it is called *designated funds*. If there is no designation, meaning the organization can allocate the funds as it chooses, it is *undesignated* funds. When a contributor sends a charity money and does not direct where to allocate the funds, the company can distribute it as they see fit. An undesignated fund donation was made.

When someone designates the funds by writing it on a donation card, online, etc., they expect their instructions to be followed. When the receiving or recipient organization does not comply, their actions can become problematic and suggest integrity concerns. This scenario is another example of why it is imperative to have a Compliance program in place. Having a robust Compliance program in place will ensure that policies and procedures are being followed and that the organization practices fiscal responsibility.

Historically, non-profit organizations focused on mission rather than margin. Additionally, vision was included as part of the strategy. Unfortunately, some non-profit organizations cut corners in their financial and operational areas because mission, vision, and value are usually the main focus. It was not unusual to hear non-profit leadership say they can't afford to have a compliance program. They would say, "We don't have enough money in the budget to do this." Such response lets me know they have failed to understand they could not afford not to invest in compliance.

Non-profit organizations should not wait to be under a microscope and scrutinized due to a scandal because they did not take the time to implement a compliance plan and program. It would be prudent to hire someone or appoint someone in the organization who could fulfil the compliance officer role. Establishing a team that includes a compliance committee can be a valuable asset.

The compliance department views every department as its customer and as such must work with them. For example, a compliance officer or someone from the compliance department can work with the leadership of finance or any other departments having issues to help them create a protocol. The process would concentrate on reporting the results of a compliance audit, e.g. billing, revenue cycle, or document the audit since the findings can affect the organization's bottom line.

In terms of fiscal responsibility, the compliance department staff should understand all. How can the compliance department audit a program to ensure all requirements including documentation are available? Consider a behavioral health provider that submits bills to Medicaid. If the compliance department staff does not understand the billing requirements or what the services entail, how can they perform an effective audit? Before an audit is performed, there must be a complete understanding of the services provided, regulatory requirements, internal systems, and staff responsible for approving and submitting claims. The compliance staff should be able to monitor every departments' internal processes.

The compliance department should work closely with the finance department. Anytime something is uncovered through an audit with financial implications it should be reported immediately to the Chief Financial Officer (CFO). Depending on the finding, the compliance auditor or officer might say: "We have a concern. It looks like there are several million dollars that can't be accounted for." This type of auditing is time sensitive and finance must be contacted especially since they would have to report to their board of directors, banks or with whomever they are required to share such status. For transparency, make sure that the financial viability of a program or service, or department within a company is always known.

When an external agency, funder, or government official comes knocking to audit your records, always be prepared. Depending on the industry, when and if you receive money from the government for providing a service, the expectation is you can be audited anytime. When I worked in corporate, my philosophy was to get each client to a place that when somebody came to perform an audit they wouldn't panic, and the auditors would be actually welcomed. How awesome would that feel? You put the work in and now a system is working. Is it perfect? It is not perfect, but you don't have to be terrified of external auditors because you don't know what skeletons will jump out the closet. Organizations that are proactive don't mind auditors coming. It's the people of organizations who are always reactive that become nervous when they are being audited or scrutinized.

If you remember one thing from reading this chapter let it be this:

If you have a business and are generating income, having a Compliance program is not an option, it is a must and size does not matter.

Real Life Examples of Break Down in Compliance Programs and Implementation

I was mortified when watching the news and saw the passenger being dragged off an airplane. Later, I learned he had a broken nose and teeth because the airline wanted one of their employees to have his seat. This passenger was a doctor; he had paid for his seat and because the plane was oversold – something that is more common than the public may be aware of - they removed the doctor from the plane. The video footage and the pictures spoke volumes about the airline's compliance policies or lack thereof. Since the incident occurred and the public's outcry for justice, the airlines are scrambling to develop and implement policies to address oversold planes and the need to remove passengers.

Another concerning issue affecting the airline industry involve service animals and pets. I understand and support the need for emotional support animals; however, I don't want to sit in a seat next to a snake because that's somebody's emotional support animal. Two separate cases involved a peacock and another feathered bird. Passengers in both situations tried to take the birds on a plane and claimed they were emotional support animals. Passengers are buying seats for these *exotic* 'emotional support' animals. It is apparent the airlines industry had to come up with criteria, policies, and procedures to address emotional support animals flying with passengers in the main cabin.

The cliché "When it rains it pours," came to hold true for the airline industry. Right after the stories broke about the doctor being removed from the plane and the issues regarding service/emotional support animals, a story was reported in the news that discussed how passengers on planes, especially on long flights, have been sexually assaulted by other passengers. In one instance, a passenger called over the flight attendant, but the flight attendant didn't know how to handle the situation. I cannot imagine someone feeling comfortable enough to violate another passenger's rights and space. The incident upset me because I fly internationally quite a bit. I thank God I have never been violated in this manner. For the airlines that do not have them, they should implement policies and procedures that address misconduct and criminal behavior while in the air. Some airlines have policies and claim to enforce them when appropriate. Airlines have reported they need help with jurisdiction concerns. When a passenger is assaulted the policies should be in accordance with laws regarding sexual harassment; it shouldn't matter if a victim/person is on the ground or is being groped in the air.

Recently, a woman reported a man was inappropriately touching her. She rung the bell for the flight attendant and received this response: "*Oh, oh that's just so and so.*" The culprit passenger was a frequent flyer with the airline. I was stunned; the staff knew the man and expressed no concern over his indecent and criminal behavior. The aforementioned example supports why having standards and policies along with complying with laws and regulations in the airline industry are non-negotiable.

The flight attendant(s) on these flights may not have previously experienced reports of sexual assault or other deviant behavior, but now they should have access to comprehensive policies that include education and training for employees which should be ongoing.

The pharmaceutical industry is guided by legal and regulatory requirements. A colleague was a VP of Compliance for a well-known pharmaceutical company. His territory included Asia and China, which was his main hub. In preparing for his first visit to China, he studied the culture which included business etiquette. The senior executive visited some of the labs where pharmaceuticals were manufactured. According to him, every time he visited, they tried to give him gifts. Initially, he felt very uncomfortable because the USA has a law called the **Foreign Corrupt Practices Act of 1977.** The law is known primarily for two of its main provisions; one that addresses accounting transparency requirements under the Securities Exchange Act of 1934 and another concerning bribery of foreign officials. His primary concern was to avoid the appearance of activity that could be perceived or interpreted as malfeasance.

The custom in China is to give gifts and to not accept them can be offensive. He learned that giving gifts was their way of showing kindness; it was their custom and culture. My colleague's employer's policies addressed gifts and that's what he followed.

Once upon a time when I worked in the insurance industry, we had pharmaceutical representatives who wanted to come on-site because we had an outpatient psychiatric facility. The representative would treat everyone to lunch and/or they would send us lunch. Their strategy was to present information about their drugs that dealt with schizophrenia, bipolar, and other mental health illnesses or issues. Not only would they buy lunch, but they would also bring gifts such as large umbrellas, hats, t-shirts, tickets to events, portfolios, etc. Over the years, the regulations have been revised and pharmaceutical representatives can no longer just give gifts without going through a process. Pharmaceutical companies had to work with their compliance department to develop policies, procedures, Codes of Conduct that address their position on giving.

Email Best Practices: Lack of Training/Ignorance or Complete Disregard of Policies and Procedures

We have witnessed compliance issues in the political arena with the famous Senator Hillary Clinton's email scandal. Clearly, one can see how the mistake can be made without meaning to, right? Many people have a business Gmail account and a personal Gmail account setup, so they can send both personal or business emails without having to log in and log out from each account every time. Unfortunately, many people have their email accounts set up this way but fail to double check which email address they are sending the email from before they hit the send button. Basic best business practice recommends to no comingle personal emails with business emails.

There are companies that allow employees to access their personal email at work while others do not. It is important for an organization to have policies that address the use and/or accessing personal email, business email, including sending business email to personal email addresses. An employee can violate laws when emailing certain files to a home or personal email accounts. For example, it is inappropriate for staff to email files containing protected health information to their home or personal email accounts. Why? Because doing so, constitutes a HIPAA violation.

Based on my experience, when these instances occur, employees are not intentionally and maliciously violating policy or regulations. It can be that an employee wants to work on a file from home to meet a deadline, but the employer provided no safe way for them to have access outside of the office. An employee may feel they have no choice but to circumvent the system. I am guilty of that very infraction myself; I have sent files from my work email to my personal email before the updated HIPAA laws. Also, the company I worked for required us to log into the system via their VPN system (Virtual Private Network). The VPN connection was troublesome; it would take a long time to connect. I usually had deadlines to meet and I could not allow a bad VPN connection to delay me.

I recall a situation while working with a client. They require all consultants to use a company laptop, so they gave me a company laptop for security purposes. I know better; I am a compliance officer, but I was working on a report and it had to be completed by a certain time. They came to me at the last minute to do something for them and I needed to print documents but could not. It was a huge file and I needed to review the hard copy. I called the client and my contact at the company; she tried to get their IT Department to help me but to no avail. I called the IT Department after hours, and unfortunately, the IT Department was not open and did not have a representative available 24-hours a day. I had to make a decision and several thoughts were in my head. "I have to get this project completed; I gave my word it would be done. I'm being paid to do this. What do I do?" I could not print the document unless I emailed the file to my Gmail email account and use my personal office printer. The client did not give me a printer when they provided the laptop.

I was in a tight situation. The client needed the project completed and I had to decide; my competence and integrity were on the line. I looked through the document to determine if there were any violations of HIPAA, trade secrets listed, or proprietary information provided. When I realized the answer to every question was no, I sent the document to my personal email, finished the project and met the deadline.

Subsequently, I received an email from the director who sub-contracts work to me requesting I review an attached document submitted by their compliance officer. The compliance officer reprimanded me because of the email incident. I contacted both the director and compliance officer and explained my position. I admitted I knew of their policy and hated I was placed in the position where I had to make an executive decision that violated their policy. I explained that if there had been trade secrets in the document, HIPAA, or anything like that, I wouldn't have done it. I had to make a decision because their IT staff left at 5:00 PM. I was working on their project after business hours. I asked the compliance officer: "What would you have me do since the company needed my report first thing in the morning? What would you have preferred I do when I couldn't reach anybody, and I tried for several days to get this rectified?"

The aforementioned situation demonstrates it is imperative that an organization provide a mechanism/system for employees to do their job whether in the office, traveling, or from home if inclement weather or some other reason occurs that keeps them out of the office.

The client suggested I could have connected their laptop to my personal printer! I was surprised and responded: "You had an issue with me sending emails to my personal email so that I could print the document to meet your deadline. Why wouldn't you have a problem with me connecting your equipment into my personal printer? I don't want to co-mingle personal and business equipment." I could not believe they suggested I should have connected their laptop to my personal printer.

Dear organization and leadership, if you want your staff to play the game, you must tell them the rules and provide a way for them to comply with those rules and requirements.

7

NEW COMPLIANCE PROGRAMS & WHY MAINTENANCE IS A MUST!

Regardless of whether an organization has a compliance officer, monitoring the Compliance program with routine maintenance is a must. An experienced compliance consultant can be both beneficial and an asset that should be considered. When an organization is implementing a new compliance program, experts recommend performing ongoing concurrent audits of operations, e.g. key systems, job functions, and documentation to name a few to confirm that training was successful. Over time, this type of monitoring can position the compliance department for a return on investment (ROI). A compliance consultant could return to the company as necessary on a per-engagement basis or be kept on retainer as needed.

What happens during audits? This is a broad question and the answer is, it depends on the type of audit; there are many kinds. In the case of a follow-up audit, a compliance officer would conduct a review or another audit to test the findings and to verify the departments are following through with the recommended and established guidelines. When companies take advantage of maintenance packages, they usually see a higher rate of compliance (fewer errors, violations, and/or fines).

Every time I work with an organization to implement a new compliance program or audit an existing one, I recommend continuing the monitoring process. Why? For the program to succeed, companies must continue the process. Compliance is a journey and not a sprint. To be realistic, companies will never have 100 percent accuracy all the time. Although technology is wonderful, and there are endless systems and platforms for companies to choose from, human beings are involved in the process. The results? There will always be errors, so one goal should be to eliminate problems and/or minimize them. When I say problems, I mean risks. Risks should be mitigated or eliminated whenever possible. Thus, my recommendation for continued monitoring.

Companies will continuously experience improvement as long as they are maintaining effective systems that include performing concurrent audits. The audit should evaluate efficiency, effectiveness, workflows, financial systems, and the compliance program.

Companies that want to improve their systems MUST audit and assess what is in place. Of course, an organization can't fix anything if they do not know something is broken. Moreover, the organization can't know anything is broken if they do not look. Before using "don't ask don't tell" as an excuse for not knowing violations or responsibilities, remember, just because you don't look it doesn't mean there are no problems. Routine monitoring and auditing should become the norm and I recommend companies identify qualified employees and train them. Additionally, it is a good idea to contract an external consultant to perform those tasks, one who is independent and objective; when employees are too close to their processes; they can miss errors.

When a company makes major operational changes in response to a failed audit and perhaps, loss of revenue, I recommend leadership assures internal monitoring is part of the risk assessment and is ongoing. It would be a good idea to have an external consultant conduct another audit within six-months to assess progress. Depending on the nature and extent of the critical findings, I recommend an external audit be performed within three-months.

A three-month check-up can summarize how the new or upgraded systems are doing. Based on the results, a six or twelve-month assessment may be necessary. Once an organization has "successful" audits over time, they can contemplate phasing out continuous audits by external consultants. A successful audit means the results show marked improvement, no new infractions, and no paybacks. Currently, I am working with a client doing well; I recommended they have an external compliance audit every two years.

AN EXTERNAL COMPLIANCE CONSULTANT

The consultant should perform an audit of the entire Compliance program to assess proper adherence to recognized best practices. At the conclusion of a contract with an external consultant consider hiring them on retainer. Most of my clients have me on retainer. When a client hires me on a retainer basis, they can schedule telephone consultations whenever they have questions or problems. I have been asked to attend meetings with government officials, attorneys, state regulators, and provide representation on behalf of companies.

When a company brings me in as part of a maintenance package, we have a contractual agreement which outlines the initiatives to take place every three to six-months (it depends on their needs). The agreement also states the tasks that will be performed while on-site, e.g. monitoring, reviewing prior audits, training records, policies, etc. Additionally, I review to confirm that the initial recommendations were acted upon and documented. When I am engaged, I come in ready to ask MANY questions that will assist me when I perform a comprehensive audit. It's all about checks and balances.

My retainer contracts usually last a year but can run longer depending on the needs of the company and the complexity of their situation. I have had companies keep me on retainer for six-months. However, I have seen the greatest growth and improvement realized for the clients that choose the one to two-year package. While other clients rather take advantage of my services on an as-needed basis.

As part of our services at One Accord Consulting Firm, there are many options to work with companies that require our assistance; the process varies per company, engagement, and industry. During the initial meeting and assessment, the best course of action for the client is determined.

I had a client in the human services industry; they had a lot of issues when I started with them. I have been consulting with them for over a year as they are a large operation that includes over 6,000 employees across multiple states and internationally. They have a lot of programs, services, and different funders. My team is auditing every one of their programs and putting systems in place based on the findings. Education is fundamental, and we incorporate education and training to ensure the appropriate staff understands their role and responsibilities. Some of the results have been a major reduction in the potential of submitting false claims, a higher implementation rate, and eliminated risks. Subsequently, they need not worry about paying back money to funders for services they have provided.

I acquired another client through the attorney of an organization. At the onset, I could tell something was not right. The president of the company was arrogant and elusive. Every time I interviewed him it was like pulling teeth to get information. The engagement was difficult due to the lack of commitment from the president and cooperation of key senior leadership. My final report indicated the best solution for them would be to develop and implement a compliance program. The Seven Elements for Effective Compliance that was previously discussed and is part of the United States Sentencing Commission's guidance for providers of Medicare and Medicaid services was used during the assessment.

The president always appeared to be angry and/or agitated while I was there. Through staff interviews, I learned that his wife had a sister company and both companies shared some of the same staff. I explained to the president that sharing staff with his wife's company was a problem IF, only IF they were both billing the government during the same time with the same staff. I made recommendations and continued to probe and ask questions. He took offense to my questions because he felt I alleged he was engaged in fraudulent activity.

He never answered the questions presented to him; I specifically asked him: "Is this happening or not?" I advised him that I made an observation and was trying to help him. I explained the staff's concern was something that I noticed during the assessment process. "You should be happy that I picked up on this." At the conclusion of the engagement, I recommended a maintenance package. I was not surprised when the president did not engage my company for the contract. Subsequently, his attorney contacted me because of additional issues. Unfortunately, there was nothing I could do; the engagement had ended. In the end, I gave them a robust Compliance Package.

As far as I know, the client didn't implement any of my suggestions; the president thought he knew everything. The reason I was there was because of their monitoring issues. Their attorney stated there were some other issues. I never knew the extent of their additional problems as I had had no further contact with them.

My advice to leadership is **do not bury your head in the sand. Answer the questions to the best of your ability especially when,** 'the innocent has nothing to hide. If you have nothing to hide, there is no reason to become offended, it is best to cooperate.

Moreover, it is important to understand when an external compliance consultant is engaged, they are there to support the organization per the contract. The compliance consultant is not your enemy and should not be treated as such.

I have never signed a contract that stated I would not report my findings. When problems are identified, I'm obligated to tell leadership; that is what they pay me to do. The expectation is that I not only find problems but create strategies to solve them. It is fair to say most of my clients contract me because they want to become compliant, otherwise, I wouldn't be there.

There are certain allegations I must report as a mandated reporter, for example, when it involves children. During one of my previous engagements, while I was reviewing reports and assessments that involved children, there were allegations of abuse. I was unable to locate any documentation or communication that the allegations were reported to the appropriate authorities. When I immediately told management, they advised me the files were in another place. The allegations involved child abuse; therefore, I was considered a mandated reporter. Luckily for them, they had the reports in another place because otherwise I would have had to report it if they didn't.

Besides my responsibility to report allegations of child abuse, there is also the ethical part. Aside from the law, I must consider my own integrity and ask myself: "Is this something they are going to report? If not, I must report it."

8

NO MORE BACKDOOR WHISTLEBLOWING

histleblowing occurs when someone witnesses, hears, sees or knows of any misconduct or wrongdoing. Employees should report any violation of a law or regulation. No more backdoor whistleblowing; you might be wondering what this means. No backdoor whistleblowing is when employees feel safe and good about reporting allegations of misconduct, negligence or illegal acts that employees, including upper management, might be committing. The corporate culture should tolerate no malfeasance or wrongdoing.

How can companies create an ethical culture? How can organizations make whistleblowing something that is no longer taboo or something that is feared? Whistleblowing can be viewed as positive because employees know change takes place when they report misconduct. They know their leadership is actively listening, and their job is not in jeopardy if and when they complete a report.

So, let's start from the beginning, **whistleblowing is when an employee or employees officially report possible acts of misconduct, fraud, inappropriate behavior, and/or any activity deemed out of alignment with a company's mission, vision,**

and values and laws of their city, country or state. Certain companies that receive money from the government must have whistleblowing guidelines in place as outlined in the Deficit Deduction Reduction Act.

Whistleblowing guidelines should be posted where all employees have access. Educating employees on policies, procedure, codes of conduct among other things are contributing factors to an organization's success. An example is training employees how to report violations via a reporting system or protocol. The culture should promote zero tolerance for misconduct or wrongdoing. Also, when they see something, they are obligated to say something.

My experience is most companies do not want to educate employees about whistleblowing guidelines/policies. They may have policies and procedures that indicate support, however, they don't want their employees going outside of the organization to report anything. Leadership prefers that employees communicate and report internally first and give the organization a chance to correct the problem before contacting an outside agency. I agree with leadership's position; they should have an opportunity to address and correct issues.

There are laws that protect the whistleblower from retaliation, firing, or any retributions stemming from them reporting.

Let me share a real-life whistleblowing example. I was working for a company which, at the time, was one of the largest insurance companies, in the area. My position interacted with Medicare professional services, corporate public relations, and staff services.

My job entailed traveling all throughout western Pennsylvania; I worked with senators, congressional staff and their constituents. I worked with medical societies, trade associations, Durable Medical Equipment providers (DME), and physicians in my territory. Anytime there were changes to Medicare and the Federal Register, I would have to apprise my group of the changes to billing, how to get their claims paid and anything else they needed to do to get a resolution.

When I held this position, a husband and wife team from California was hired. It was interesting because I later found out that they would move around to different companies and whenever they were hired by a company, they came together as a package deal. They came and learned the inner workings of the organization, the billing system, and every deficiency. Subsequently, they became whistleblowers regarding their discoveries. They received millions of dollars in a settlement because they reported their findings to the government due to Medicare fraudulent claims. Usually, the settlement is determined by the money the company must refund to the government and can be calculated based on audit findings and other factors discovered in the investigation.

If a company must pay back $50,000,000 depending on the industry, the whistleblowers (in this case the husband and wife team) could get up to 30% of the money the company pays the government. The Security and Exchange Commission (SEC) issued the largest rewards for whistleblowers under the Dodd-Frank Act, setting a new record at more than $33 million according to Sylvan Lane from the TheHill.Com

There are Four Qui Tam Laws that provide those who 'blow the whistle' with monetary rewards for reporting fraud or illegal activity are:

1. False Claims Acts
2. IRS Whistleblower Reward Program
3. The Securities Whistleblower Reward Program
4. Commodity Exchange Act Whistleblower Rewards

The couple received a hefty reward because of what they reported. They found out some of the things the company was doing inappropriately and doing wrong in the system and then they reported it to the government. From what was reported, the couple was not new to whistleblowing; the story is they made reports like the one I described two other times.

This couple identified ALL the issues, violations and brokenness within the system rather quickly. The question kept surfacing: "Why didn't the leadership over the responsible departments find those issues?" Maybe they did not want to find the problems because it was suspected the activities were intentional.

During the time this was taking place, the company was switching over from paper claims processing to electronic billing. The Center for Medicare and Medicaid Services (CMS) was providing monetary incentives and other resources to facilitate the new initiative and to encourage providers to embrace electronic billing, especially in rural areas. The investigation discovered that someone in upper management created a system that would count electronic claims twice; it appeared as though twice the number of electronic claims were being processed. Therefore, management were reaching the goals of getting the providers on board. Everything looked wonderful, so we all received bonuses. Senior management took us to a fabulous restaurant for a celebratory luncheon. Unfortunately, the celebration was short-lived. It was reported that a certain member in leadership had manipulated the billing system. Eventually, he was demoted and relocated to another department within the company.

Although he was not immediately terminated, he was let go not long after the transfer. Who all knew what was going on? Anybody that worked in the system and on the electronic data interchange project should have known in addition to the business analyst who tested the system and monitored the billing and claims processing system should have been able to sense something was wrong. The company never took the money back from the staff who received bonuses; we had nothing to do with the scheme. How would we know? There was no doubt about the gross misconduct going on and it was one of the thing that the whistleblowing couple uncovered. The husband just happened to work in the staff services Department, and he was a technology guru. He had direct access to the system and was knowledgeable about the technology surrounding the project.

This whistleblowing story is a perfect example of how a company would have benefited from someone reporting internally their suspicions of misconduct. Perhaps, employees were afraid to report even if they did not know exactly what was wrong. It is important for organizations to establish protocols that assure reports of wrongdoing go to a neutral party or department. Can you imagine what would have happened if someone had to report to the corrupt manager? It may not have been good for the employee(s) alleging fraud.

A standard for organizations to embed in their culture is transparency. I am aware transparency is a word that is thrown around a lot. We hear about transparency in government, in corporate America, on Wall Street, and in the stock market. "But, do people really want transparency? Do organizations really want transparency? Do the powers that be really care?" Those are questions a company's leadership can and should answer. It is important for them to assess if they want transparency; do they want their companies to run well, have a reputation of integrity, and provide great products and services? If they do, then they should establish a culture where employees feel empowered and more than willing to report misconduct.

It doesn't matter what role an employee holds in an organization; every person and position is essential. All employees should be made to feel like they are part of the company and on a team that shares common goals. When new employees come on board, they should be well trained and educated on the company's mission, vision, values, and code of conduct. As soon as they come through the door, let them know what the expectations are and that they are an essential part of the process. Continue to remind them of the following, "You are an essential part of the compliance process and we need you to continue making this company the success that it is. Please know that we have ZERO tolerance in our organization for misconduct." Make it very clear and have your code of conduct accessible. Make sure your organization discusses not only the importance of having an ethical culture during onboarding and New Employee Orientation (NEO) but also continues to remind employees all year-round because often they may forget. Remember, employees come and go, leadership changes, and laws and regulations change; always keep people abreast of what's going on.

I believe if leaders establish and build a culture around ethics and integrity and encourage employees to report misconduct with an assurance there would not be retaliation, there would be a decline in some of the egregious stories we have read and heard in the news. My experience with leadership is that most can't get past the who; they are adamant to know who reported. I incessantly ask leadership: "Why does it matter to you **WHO** reported it to me? What should matter to you is if what was reported is true. Is what was reported true? Why is it important to know who reported the issue?" When I ask those questions, most of the time upper management gets the picture and stops pushing to get names. There will always be employees who make false reports because they are disgruntled. This is a negative side of allowing anonymous reporting. A company's policy should encourage employees to make good faith reports and include disciplinary action for those who abuse the system by making false reports.

To recap, building a culture of ethics and integrity, zero tolerance for misconduct, and making employees/people feel essential could eliminate fear of retaliation; causing employees to report. Employees may be inclined to report their good faith report if they believe their efforts will be taken seriously. On the other hand, it is inappropriate for employees who use the system, you know the type: "*I hate my boss. I don't like my supervisor, so, I'll use this reporting system to get back at them and cause trouble.*" No, we don't tolerate that either. However, if you establish a culture of positive responses to people reporting and zero tolerance for misconduct, employees may not hesitate to report.

I have worked with clients who subscribed to building an ethical culture and implementing policies and procedures that supported the initiative. These clients saw an increase in the number of reports filed. This should not be seen as negative because, in actuality, employees are following policy. They are reporting what they believe to be a problem. The ethical culture encourages employees to come to you first, so you can correct the problem as opposed to them going outside. You may not have to deal with a potential visit from an external auditor such as the Office of Inspector General (OIG) or the Attorney General (AG) office.

I feel strongly about establishing an ethical culture; one of the first things I do when I am engaged to help organizations develop or assess their Compliance program and plan, is to review their code of conduct, and policies regarding professionalism, reporting misconduct, and whistleblowing (if they have them). The code of conduct must be part of every company's Compliance program and Plan. As we know, every organization is different. The Code of conduct is drafted or shaped by senior leadership; it serves as a guide for the Compliance Department to provide monitoring and oversight of the company's Compliance program.

How do we expect our employees to conduct themselves in the workplace? The Human Resources (HR) Department usually works closely with the Compliance Department especially for enforcing the Code of Conduct. The code addresses professionalism in the workplace and HR follows all policies to address employee behavior. For example, when it comes to politics, employees should know how they are to conduct themselves. Policies that address things like lobbying for political parties or candidates on behalf of the organization must be shared with all employees. For example, an employee is very active in their political party's activities. Of course, the company cannot prohibit participation, however, the organization's policy stipulates the employee can't use the company's name to represent their thoughts and opinions on politics.

Every organization that I've worked with have had their own policies regarding political and community affiliations, there have been standards on how these organizations expect employees to conduct themselves; some standards emphatically stated absolutely no accepting of kickbacks, no fraud, waste, and abuse, or tolerance for any form of harassment. Additionally, these organizations' standards address employees traveling on behalf of the company, HIPAA, confidentiality, information technology, and safety concerns, etc. Although most Codes of conduct contain similar features based on industry standards language, the code should be tailored to a company's ethical culture. One size does not fit all.

See the Reference Section at the End of the Book for Additional Resources.

RIPPED FROM THE HEADLINES

What can we learn from the news reports on corporate malfeasance, CEO scandals, and allegations of gross misconduct? If you are a business or individual looking at those cases, what can you learn? I think we can agree that many things went wrong. We can question whether or not these companies had a compliance program and if so, why wasn't it enforced?

How can misconduct go undetected for prolonged periods of time? What went wrong in the Bernie Madoff case? The Securities and Exchange Commission (SEC) had looked at Madoff's operation and missed the red flags. Where were the checks and balances? Bernie Madoff initially got away with a lot. Both of his sons denied knowing anything about his schemes. How could that be? Both of his sons worked very closely with him, yet it is possible they did not know. Mrs. Madoff was interviewed and categorically denied knowing what her husband was doing.

We know that people can be good at hiding things. Again, there are individuals and companies that want to be honest; they go out of their way to be transparent. Why should a company want to have a compliance program? When there is a compliance program, a responsible person such as a compliance officer is in charge of auditing, monitoring and providing oversight of the business. The program supports the company's endeavors to meet regulatory and legal compliance and discourages all violations.

Bernie Madoff would not have gotten away with what he did unless there were others who were in cahoots with him willing to cover up and look the other way. Also, having a robust and enforced Compliance program in place could have helped to detect his illegal activities sooner and/or deterred him from willingly committing fraud. It is wishful thinking to believe having an active Compliance program and providing employees with the ability to report wrongdoing would have helped catch Mr. Madoff much earlier. Why? Because according to a story in *The Telegraph* UK article, there was evidence of misconduct dating to the 1970s. You can read the full article here: http://bit.ly/integritymatters-madoff.

In April of 2018, CNN put together a Bernie Madoff timeline outlining impressive figures and the demise of his empire. The article claims 16,519 investors filed claims against him. To read more about Bernie Madoff's son Andrew go to: http://bit.ly/integrity-matters-madofftimeline.

The timeline reads like a sad fictional story; however, unfortunately, it is true. In 2010, his son Mark Madoff, who was only 46, committed suicide and four years later his other son Andrew died of cancer at 48.

Another article on Forbes.com talks about Madoff's impossible returns and says the returns: "Should have been a major warning signal but unfortunately, many fell for his Ponzi scheme." Read the entire article here: http://bit.ly/integritymatters-madoff-ponzyscheme.

The pyramid scheme was an elaborate one and secretive. The '*Business Insider*' website posted an article describing how it worked. Bernie Madoff would convince investors to invest, promising and guarantying unusually high returns. Then, he would encourage the investors to leave their money invested so they could earn even more money. Meanwhile, the new investments were used to pay returns to older investors. The person behind the scheme pockets the extra money or uses it to expand the operation." You can read the rest of the article here: http://bit.ly/integritymatters-madoff-ponzischeme.

Due to the Ponzi scheme and its aftermath, there were many changes made to the way companies are monitored. Some of the governmental entities that should have detected Madoff's scheme received reprimands. The Securities and Exchange Commission (SEC) had to explain how they missed it since they audited his operation. "How did you overlook certain things? Why didn't you address these issues back then?" These were some of the questions the SEC were charged with answering. The SEC had to make significant changes within their organization. You can see those changes in this article: http://bit.ly/integritymatters-changes.

Due to the organizations and people who looked the other way, thousands of people lost their life's savings and some committed suicide. Until Madoff was caught, he got away with trust fraud, mail fraud, wire fraud, money laundering, making false statements, and perjury. Bernie Madoff was arrested on December 11, 2008, convicted in 2009, and sentenced to 150 years in federal prison. They estimated the size of his fraud to be 64.8 billion dollars.

The US Securities and Exchange Commission was also criticized for not investigating Madoff more thoroughly. Reports suggested the agency received allegations as early as 1999 but didn't follow up. Think about all the people, over 4,800 clients he had ripped off; the saddest part of this story is that he could have been stopped much sooner.

Peter Madoff, his brother, was the senior managing director and Chief Compliance officer at Bernard L. Madoff Investment Securities. Peter's daughter, Shana Madoff was the firm's Rules and Compliance officer and attorney. Looking at the people he appointed in key oversight positions it is clear Madoff didn't want to be transparent; transparency would not have benefited his scheme.

THE IMPORTANCE OF BOARD GOVERNANCE

Forming a corporation and electing a board of directors is a legal process stipulated by the state where the corporation incorporates. Each state has different rules and requirements for establishing various organizations, such as a C-Corporation. However, all for-profit and non-profit corporations are required by law to have boards of directors.* The state where an organization incorporates determines when and how many directors are required.

How active is the board? Does the leadership have the board wrapped around their fingers? Is it a volunteer board? Are board members paid? I have had discussions with people who think board members act differently when compensated for their board appointment. This belief can suggest that board members who are compensated may compromise policies or laws. I disagree because not every board member that gets paid to be on a board is unethical; I don't believe it. There are aberrations to most things, so it's possible to have a board member look the other way because they are getting paid to be on the board.

Who needs an extra layer of monitoring and oversight? In every company, especially if they want to eliminate risks and maximize compliance, an engaged board of directors can serve as another set of eyes. There is value in having a robust Compliance program that demonstrates routine monitoring. Organizations can benefit from voluntarily implementing a program; it is always better to be proactive instead of reactive. The attitude of every business culture should be preemptive – do before it is mandated.

RIPPED FROM THE HEADLINES

Cynthia Cooper, the former Chief Audit Executive for World-Com, discussed in her book: *Extraordinary Circumstances*, what happened when she realized that something was not right with the financial entries of WorldCom. The more she reviewed entries and asked questions, the more she became concerned. Like other people, some of Cynthia's colleagues were advised to block her efforts when she tried to audit the company's books and records. She confirms the charge: "When you see something, say something." Cynthia's story helps readers understand why it is important to stand for what is right, the consequences of "doing the right thing," why ethics and integrity matter, and the process for reporting misconduct.

In 2002, WorldCom was a growing telecom giant headquartered in Clinton, Mississippi. WorldCom's president was Bernie Ebbers and he had grown the company through acquisition. Unfortunately, WorldCom would make history as being labeled as the: "largest fraud in corporate history" (Cooper, 2008). They intentionally falsified their financial statements for over a year by $11 billion.

I, like Cynthia Cooper, believe that: "All ethical decision-making is not forged and the crossroads of major events but start in childhood, decision by decision and brick by brick" (Cooper, 2008). It is important for Leadership to understand the leader. An organization's culture should have zero tolerance for any misconducts regardless of who is responsible.

THE DEFICIT REDUCTION ACT, DRA

The act of 2005, granted flexibility to states to modify Medicaid programs that could negatively affect children and families and their access to care.

The DRA created a center for state fraud and abuse, and this goes back to false claims: *If a state enacts a false claim act, that is closely molded on the federal version of the law, the federal government will increase the state share of amounts recovered under that false claim.* The DRA covers other services but for the most part, it is the government's position requiring states who provide Medicaid and Medicare services to enact and abide by the False Claims Act. This applies to those organizations that make claims for reimbursement for services to the government.

Part of the functions of the DRA was to require organizations to have whistleblowing guidelines in place and that those guidelines be shared with all employees.

Organizations should look at the DRA as a guide whether they are in the health care industry or not. Much of the information can serve as a valuable resource for any industry. Don't reinvent the wheel, take advantage of the resource.

9

PERSONAL SELF-COMPLIANCE

What is self-compliance? Self-Compliance is how you take care of what you do, what you say, and how the principles you have learned are applied in your life and business. Even if you have no company, how does self-compliance apply daily?

I am a woman of faith, and a lot of if not everything that I believe in terms of my views, thoughts, ideologies, and philosophy about how one should conduct themselves, extends to the moral foundation I get through the Word of God. There are many stories throughout the scriptures with references that tie to ethics, morality, and integrity. It is a fact when you work in Corporate America or are an entrepreneur, not all customers or clients are going to be people of faith. The point is you may not know because the conversation of religious views and preferences does not come up. Some companies have policies that limit conversations about religious views and/or affiliations. I don't have to go into a workplace and say what I am or who I am; my actions and the way I conduct myself in business should speak to that. There will always be someone or persons who will try to attack and/or undermine a person's integrity.

The people I interact with will recognize that I operate from a place of ethics and integrity. The way I conduct business and the notion of transparency will also be apparent to them. When I'm working with clients, part of the discovery process is finding out the answers to the following: "What's the culture here? Are you open to change? Do you promote and encourage honest communication? Do you subscribe to transparency or do you push people to cover up wrong-doing? Do you want employees to report problems to you, so you can fix them, and do what is right?" Those are some questions I ask my new clients. I teach entrepreneurs and people I mentor that integrity matters. You must be your word. You must do what you say you will do. When you do not follow through on your word, you are labeled as untrustworthy. A harsh word and description for it is liar.

My perspective and thought of self-compliance are about establishing a plan with strategies for your life, goals, aspirations, and dreams and doing what is necessary to comply with your plan.

What plans do you have for yourself and/or your family? Toward the end of a calendar year, many people create vision boards; they come up with strategic plans for their business, self-and/or families. Even though a collective goal may exist for the family, every person in the family has a role and responsibility to uphold. If someone fails to do their part, it could change the dynamics as far as the end goals for that family go. I give these examples when I'm speaking with clients about the concept of self-compliance.

If a husband and wife have a plan to build or purchase a new home within a two to three-year period, they should clearly understand what they have to do to achieve their goal. Both parties must be committed to the plan.

For starters, the plan might be to pay off all their debt and save a specific amount of money within a particular period. Part of their plan might be to not purchase anything above a certain amount without the approval of the other person.

One day the wife goes to the mall with a friend and notices that Neiman Marcus has an amazing sale going on and the items are "too good" to pass up. She comes home with a boatload of clothes; albeit, they were on sale. The problem is that she does not exercise self-compliance and did not honor her word. The wife agreed not to make any purchases over a certain amount of dollars without the approval of her husband.

On the other hand, the husband is an avid antique car lover. While visiting one of his friends he learns his buddy has one of his dream cars up for sale. He had been eyeing the car for over a year and now the price of the car was reduced by 15%. He does the SAME thing his wife did. The whole notion of self-compliance went out the window. When operating outside of a corporate environment, exercising self-compliance is necessary for success. We all must abide by someone's rules and laws. There are laws of nature, laws in any industry we operate in, including laws for those who are in ministry, especially in the church/faith-based organization. Every religion or faith has their own precepts and requirements.

I have seen great growth in both my professional and personal life because of self-compliance. It keeps me accountable to myself and to God. Regardless of who my client is, church, non-profit, employer, or a solopreneur, I must be my word. Whatever, I say I will do for them I have to do it. So, my personal self-compliance has helped me in business because I developed a reputation for being ethical and integral. Many of my clients have come through word of mouth and/or referrals. If you think about it, I'm a little fish in this big pond yet my business is having a big impact on all the companies and businesses who contract me.

It is all about developing a reputation for ethics, a work ethic, being your word, and doing what you say you will do. If I can't do something in the time frame I said, I would, I immediately let the client know and explain why. I may offer something extra as a form of reparation for the delay. Sometimes, it's not my fault; the delay can be attributed to the client not providing the required documentation in time. I'm dealing with this very situation as I write this book.

A client asked me to perform another audit, the leadership and attorney asked me to do it by a certain date. I thought I could meet their expectations, but I'm relying on their employees in their finance department to provide me with requested invoices and records. I cannot do my part until their staff does their part. Consequently, I'm not meeting the deadline; it's not my fault. I made my client and attorney aware because communication is key. It helps to be open; having honest and effective communication has served me well.

10

THE PROOF IS IN THE PUDDING: SUCCESS STORIES

One of my favorite parts of my job is when I get to help companies thrive by avoiding losing money, services, and possibly the reputation they spent a lot of time building.

Investing money to develop or improve a current Compliance program costs money; however, when implemented, it can save companies hundreds of thousands and sometimes millions of dollars.

This chapter discusses three success stories that involved engaging me as a compliance and integrity expert/consultant. I am generally hired or contacted through a client's attorneys because they want audits done under attorney-client privilege. For example, one client had a compliance officer, but the person had limited experience, knowledge, and expertise to be in the position. The employee was literally placed in the position and expected to develop and implement a Compliance program when they did not know how to do it. To their credit, the employee tried to do the job to the best of their ability. For example, they researched and found policies and procedures that other organizations had posted online and used them. They established a system for employees to report violations of laws, regulations, misconduct, and believed the organization was complying with all the rules and regulations for their industry until the government came knocking.

According to the government, the company had been billing a particular service incorrectly for several years. Essentially, the allegation was the organization fraudulently billed the government and owed them an astronomical refund; **we are talking about millions of dollars**. As expected, the organization disagreed with the government's position and their attorney contacted me to review the situation. **After completing my audit of the program and services in question, it was determined that both the organization and government were actually at fault**. When an organization or provider agrees to take money from the government for rendering services, they must sign a document stating that they understand their responsibilities and all billing requirements.

During the audit, all the communication from the government including electronic and printed, sent to their providers was reviewed. We could not establish that effective communication had been given. For example, no certified mail had been sent, no updated information was provided on the government's website.

After auditing the company's processes and analyzing all the data, **I was able to position the organization and their corporate counsel to negotiate a reduced payback/settlement amount. Due to the audit results and findings, the penalty or payout wasn't nearly as astronomical as it could have been. To the delight of my client,** the government accepted the company's proposal and the issue was resolved once the settlement was paid.

After we took care of that problem, I worked with the company and their compliance officer to build their Compliance program and put protocols and systems in place to prevent a similar situation from happening in the future.

Another success story involves a small organization that brought me in to help them after they got into trouble with one of their companies; the client knew they needed to act quickly. The organization was so small they had no compliance officer, let alone a Compliance program in place. The company was accused of fraudulently billing the government for two years. **I immediately conducted a comprehensive review and assessment of their business practices, protocols, financial policies, and procedures.** I needed to see how they billed claims, documented their services and training, tracked employee attendance, and other key elements.

After the review, I was able to provide the client with a comprehensive report of my findings with recommendations that would assure the organization would be in compliance if followed. Additionally, my recommendations would increase their revenue, decrease errors, paybacks and maximize compliance. We were able to negotiate with the government and reached an amicable resolution. At the request of my client, I conducted a follow-up audit six-months later. The client had begun implementing the suggested recommendations. As a result, they had zero findings on a subsequent external audit the government conducted, paybacks were not required, and if those results were not encouraging enough, my client retained a profitable program. They met every regulatory criterion per the government's guideline.

The last story I'll share with you is about the leadership of a department in a human services organization. Unfortunately, they were suspected of forging documentation to meet internal performance requirements. If the allegations were deemed true it would have meant that the company was submitting false claims to the government. It's a big deal when an organization is accused of false claims; they may face fines, penalties, be placed on probation, lose their funding, or lose their program(contract) if the allegations are true. What happens to the people the organization supports and the services they provide?

I was contracted to conduct an audit covering a specific time-frame, at least two years. I had to interview key employees, including leadership, to get a better understanding of what had occurred. After I completed the audit, it was determined that inaccurate billing had occurred. However, it was done out of ignorance and not intentionally. The staff was not properly educated or trained on the appropriate billing requirements and proper documentation procedures.

After the contract started, the requirements had changed. In the process, there was a turnover in staff, and no one kept up with the billing requirements. The team responsible for billing and documenting the process and billing were doing business as usual; they were unaware of any regulatory changes.

Due to my background and expertise dealing with similar situations, I was able to work with the client's attorney and negotiated a payback schedule that was satisfactory to the government and to my client. The organization had to revisit their compliance plan and put procedures in place to prevent similar oversights and errors from happening again.

The client asked me to create a training program for their staff; we established internal audit protocols, so this type of situation didn't happen in the future. This client understood the benefit of audits and accountability, so they engaged me to audit all their programs. Their purpose was to confirm the new systems and protocols were still in place and being done correctly. I am scheduled to go back in a year to follow up and conduct another audit.

The above were three success stories from the many I have under my belt; all dealing with funding, billing documentation, and allegations of fraud. In the last story, the **management** overseeing the department at fault was removed because the senior leadership believed they should have known better. The managers should have known the guidelines and expectations that would have prevented the situation. **They allowed fraudulent claims to be billed which is a direct violation of the False Claims Act.** In the end, everything turned out for the best. Even though there were minimal paybacks, things could have been worse.

11

CONCLUSION & NEXT STEPS

Why compliance? Why ethics? Why the book? I have been in the industry, working in the compliance industry for a long time and I have seen a lot. I could write a movie about some of the situations I have experienced, and people wouldn't believe it. The good, the bad, and the ugly; I have witnessed it all. It still surprises me when I meet clients or people who are starting up businesses and don't even understand the importance of conducting research to determine their industry requirements.

Organizations must be aware of all tax laws and how they are structured. Should you be a C-Corp? Should you be an S-Corp? Are you an LLC? Do you have employees and if so, do you pay insurance and/or payroll taxes? Do you engage independent contractors? Do you issue Form 1099 to your independent contractors? When you are an entrepreneur there are things that must be done to assure compliance. What is alarming is contracting with large corporations with more than 5,000 employees; however, they have no compliance program.

As previously stated, there are certain industries that do not promote or enforce having a compliance program. I recall an engagement with a former client who submitted mental health claims to state government for reimbursement. Imagine my surprise when I discovered my client had no program in place. When I completed a compliance assessment and subsequently a comprehensive audit, I couldn't wait to help them turn things around.

I summarized my findings and checked them in a final report. When I met with the client to present the written report, I also shared: "You hired people to provide a service and you are paying people to provide that service. For the most part, you KNOW this service was and is being provided. You received monies from the state for those services. Unfortunately, the funder requested you refund the money because you don't have proper documentation, and in some situations, your staff didn't have the right credentials. Additionally, you are going to be fined over licensing issues." I never like being the bearer of bad news but that's exactly what happened.

I continued: "If you had an active Compliance program in place, a solid program, you probably wouldn't be in this current situation and certainly wouldn't have had to pay back the amount you had to pay."

It still surprises me that some senior leadership are not seeing the value of compliance. It is considered a big expense with no ROI. I had conversations with managers that indicated they can't afford the expense; however, I believe they can't afford not to invest in compliance. Through my years of experience, seeing the pitfalls and ways that businesses get into trouble, I have concluded that if organizations were to be proactive instead of reactive, they would eliminate or minimize risks.

To excel in my profession, I endeavor to stay abreast of the latest trends, research, updates, laws, and regulatory changes. I can't help my clients if I am unaware of current information. How do I stay up to date on compliance news? I subscribe to listservs, attend conferences, network with professional and trade associations, and other compliance professionals. I subscribe to compliance magazines and blogs.

I advise compliance professionals to invest in themselves. I have to invest in myself to be the best and to offer my clients the best. This can be true for businesses as well; you must make an investment in your business. I remind clients and potential clients they are going to pay now or later. It's better to pay up front than on the backend because it will probably be costlier. At that point, chances are you have citations, fines, penalties, and/or damages. This can quickly add up to three times of what it would have cost them to bring in a consultant and implement a robust compliance program.

I would rather you invest upfront, hire the right people, get external consultants to come in and make sure that your program is where it should be. There's always room for improvement but you can develop a solid Compliance program and run it like a well-oiled machine. You might receive allegations of misconduct here or there, you may miss something here or there, but at least you would not get caught off guard or be surprised when you are prepared.

Compliance officers are an asset. Besides the lengthy list of responsibilities and tasks, they can help companies increase their finances. How? Sometimes, compliance officers catch things that should have been billed for reimbursement and were not. Also, they can assist with development, expansion, and growth. A compliance officer may identify invoices that were submitted to a client, but payment was never received.

Helping organizations to avoid pitfalls, advising them how they can grow and expand their business or services, and help them keep more of the money they earn is another reason I wrote this book. Yes, companies can keep their money, and provide quality services and products; that is the main reason most went into business in the first place.

Compliance officers want to help strengthen your company, so you don't make the kind of mistakes that could threaten your reputation. Depending on the organization, when egregious acts like submitting false claims are committed, intentionally or not, the information can't be shared with the public and ultimately cause reputational harm.

Read the book, take notes, and if you do not have a compliance program in place, a compliance officer, or access to a compliance consultant, make sure you remedy that sooner rather than later.

NEXT STEPS:

Congratulations, you now know MORE about compliance than most people. How does that feel? I hope that my easy and conversational writing style did not make this book too boring but the contrary. I pray that it motivated you to take a hard look at your business/company and even your personal life.

Whether you are a solopreneur, entrepreneur, or a corporation, the first thing you need to do is to look inside: "Are we OK?" It is like doing a self-check-up and saying: "After reading this book, we *NEED* to talk. Let's sit down and talk to our leadership and compliance consultant about our company. Are we on the right path? This is what we have been doing; what do you think about this?" Those are great questions to begin the process of speaking with a compliance consultant.

Maybe you cannot wait to get some sort of pulse or status on your business. If so, you can take advantage of the complimentary assessment I have put together. It is the VERY assessment I use when I audit non-profit human services organizations. I know that is a generous gift; you are welcome.

I have various assessments because I work with different industries. As a result, NOT all the questions or sections on the complimentary assessment will apply to your industry but it is a GREAT place to start.

Request your Complimentary Assessment below:

http://www.oneaccordconsultingfirm.com/

It is my hope you take advantage of the resources in this book, whether you call *One Accord* or not, please find someone. My call to action for you is: **Take Action Today!**

I want you to look at your internal organization and ask the following hard but oh, so necessary questions:

"If external regulators came in to do an audit on our company, program, services, or products, how would we fare? Are we confident that we are doing **everything** the right way? Are we reporting correctly? Are we billing correctly? How is our customer satisfaction? Are we honoring our word? Are we doing for our customers what we said we would do?"

Thank you for purchasing and reading my book, and don't forget to request your complimentary assessment here: **http://www.oneaccordconsultingfirm.com/**

ABOUT THE AUTHOR

With over 20 years of combined experience in corporate and regulatory compliance, Dr. Robyn S. Joppy is an expert in her field.

Over the years, she has worked in both the healthcare and dental industries as well as the non-profit sector. In addition, she worked as the vice president of corporate compliance and integrity at an international human services organization and served as an integrity consultant for faith-based organizations, trade associations and more.

Dr. Robyn has always felt passionate about helping others and she finds true pleasure in connecting with others. She has conducted over 200 workshops, 100 keynote presentations, and co-authored the One Company's Perspective on Employee Education: E+E+E=E (Compliance & Ethics Professional, 2014). Her entrepreneurial spirit and extensive knowledge of the industry drove her to create the Compliance Gazette, a newsletter distributed to over 3,500 domestic and international employees on a quarterly basis.

Dr. Robyn's true passion is education and self-improvement. She is a graduate of Drexel University, Syracuse University, Pennsylvania State University, and George Washington University. Dr. Robyn believes that the key to success is continuous self-development and she is constantly seeking to learn more through public speaking engagements, compliance education and training, human resource development, mentoring and coaching, and conducting market research and analysis.

Her in-depth knowledge of national health care policies and financing issues, compliance requirements and trends, legislation and initiatives has helped her establish long-lasting relationships with some of the leading medical and professional societies, and a wide network of contacts within trade associations, congressional members, hospitals, senior citizen groups and other special interest communities.

How to connect with Dr. Robyn

http://www.oneaccordconsultingfirm.com/about-us/
LinkedIn: http://bit.ly/drjoppy-linkedin

REFERENCES SECTION

Board Governance

Basic Governance Guide for Non-Profit Organizations
Non-Profit Quarterly (NPQ): What is Governance June 9th, 2077
by the editors
http://bit.ly/integritymatters-governance

The Imperfect Board Member: Discovering the Seven Disciplines
of Governance Excellence, 18th edition Deficit Reduction Act
Mandates Education on Fraud and Whistleblowers.

Office on Inspector General US Department of Health and Human Services https://oig.hhs.gov/

Duff Victoria. "When Does a Corporation Need to Require a
Board of directors?" http://bit.ly/integritymatters-boardofdirec-
tors Accessed 06 June 2018

Code of Conducts PDF Resources

Search for: https://abc.xyz/investor/other/google-code-of-conduct.html

Starbucks: http://www.starbucks.ph/media/Business-Ethics-and-Compliance-eng_tcm70-11290.pdf
https://www.thehersheycompany.com/content/dam/corporate-us/documents/investors/code-of-conduct.pdf

Frequently asked questions regarding **Corporate Integrity Agreements** can be found at this website:
http://bit.ly/integritymatters-cia

*Church/faith-based organizations

URL: https://en.wikipedia.org/wiki/Faith-based_organization
Website Title: Faith-based organization – Wikipedia
Date Accessed: July 06, 2018

*Go to the OIG and **(Health and Human Services) HHS** website (search for: Corporate Integrity Agreement. https://oig.hhs.gov/compliance/corporate-integrity-agreements/index.asp

*Restaurant Listserv:

https://www.restaurant.org/Events-Networking/Networking-Groups/Human-Resources-and-Risk-and-Safety-Management.

*Another great place to research requirements and resources is The Compliance Office for the United States. Here is their website: https://www.compliance.gov/ If you are interested in listservs relevant to the United States Environmental Protection Agency (EPA), you could join by going to this site: https://www.epa.gov/chief/chief-listserv. The last resource I will share with you are listservs: https://www.fascrs.org/listservs and the website for the health care industry: https://healthethicstrust.com/

*Risk and Compliance:

https://riskandcompliancemagazine.com/ and https://www.complianceweek.com/ are great resources to keep handy. You can sign up to receive compliance tips daily, weekly, or as often as you prefer. (They are compliance blogs).

Tax Guide for Churches and Religious Organizations

https://bit.ly/integritymatters-taxguide

Whistleblowing PDF Resources

https://www.sec.gov/whistleblower

See in the following pages a sample of The Seven Elements of Effective Compliance.

The 7 Elements of Effective Compliance
Elements of Effective Compliance

Element 1:
Written Policies, Procedures & Standards of Conduct

Policies, procedures & standards of conduct must:

- Articulate the company's commitment to comply with all Federal and State Standards;
- Describes compliance expectations as embodied in the code of conduct;
- Implement the operation of the compliance program;
- Guide employees and others on dealing with suspected, detected or reported compliance issues;
- Identify how to communicate compliance issues to appropriate personnel;
- Describe how suspected, detected or reported compliance issues are investigated and resolved by the company; and
- Include a policy of non-intimidation and non-retaliation for good faith participation in the compliance program.

Element 2:

Compliance officer, Compliance Committee & High Level Oversight

High Level Oversight

Senior Management:

- Must be engaged in the compliance program; and
- Must recognize the importance of the compliance program in the company's success.

Compliance Officer, Compliance Committee & High Level Oversight

Role of the Compliance officer

- Develop and implement policies, procedures, and practices
- Oversees and monitors the implementation of the Compliance program
- Update and revise the program as appropriate
- Develop, coordinate, and participate in a multi-faceted training and education program
- Coordinate and participate in internal audits
- Review, respond to, and investigate reports of non-compliance
- Serve as a resource across the organization on substantive compliance questions and issues
- Have a broad knowledge of the organization and its operation and an awareness of applicable laws and regulations, and the significant risk areas for the organization

Compliance Officer, Compliance Committee & High Level Oversight

Role of the Compliance Committee

Assist the Compliance officer with oversight of procedures and systems ensuring:

- Compliance with all applicable laws and regulations;
- Employees, Officers, and Directors act in accordance with appropriate ethical standards;
- The delivery of high-quality services;
- The development of standards of conduct and policies and procedures;
- The identification of actual and potential risk areas;
- The education and training of employees;
- The establishment of confidentiality standards and requirements;
- The enhancement of current systems used to evaluate and respond to compliance issues

Element 3:

Effective Compliance Education & Training

- Continually educate all employees, Officers and Board Members
- Employees must be made aware of requirements to do their jobs well
- Effectiveness determined through compliance with all regulatory and legal requirements

Element 4:

Effective Lines of Communication

- Lines of communication must exist between the Compliance officer and others.
- Must assure confidentially
- Lines of communication must be accessible and allow for anonymous and good faith reporting of real and potential compliance issues and other violations.

Element 5:

Well-publicized Disciplinary Standards

- Implementation of procedures which encourage good faith participation in the compliance program
- Standards must include policies that:
  - ☐ Articulate expectations for reporting compliance issues and assist in their resolution
  - ☐ Identify noncompliance or unethical behavior; and
  - ☐ Provide for timely, consistent and effective enforcement of the standards when noncompliance or unethical behavior is determined.

Element 6:

Effective Systems for Routine Monitoring and Auditing

Internal Audits

Internal Audit Process:

- An internal program or system is selected to be audited.
- A sample size and timeframe are determined.
- A review is conducted of the information associated with the program system, and the individual(s) selected.
- When the audit is complete, a meeting is scheduled with the appropriate leadership and management team to review findings, scope and audit recommendations.
- The responsible department leadership is responsible for developing a corrective action plan to mitigate the issues discovered.

Effective Systems for Routine Monitoring and Auditing

Risk Assessments

Risk Assessments Must:

- Address major compliance and fraud, waste and abuse risk areas
- Be conducted for each operational area
- Be conducted at least once a year

Organizations must conduct ongoing reviews of risk areas.

Effective Systems for Routine Monitoring and Auditing

OIG Exclusions Screenings

- Guidance on Effective Compliance program s incorporates CMS requirements for organizations to screen for excluded individuals and entities
  - ☐ Individuals may be excluded by the OIG from participation in any federal health care program, including Medicaid
- Screening is to be conducted prior to hiring a new employee of contracting with an entity and then monthly thereafter

Effective Systems for Routine Monitoring and Auditing

- Organizations must establish and implement an effective system for routine monitoring and identification of compliance risks.
- Organizations must have an auditing work plan that addresses its risks and is coordinated, overseen and/ or executed by the Compliance officer with assistance from the Compliance Department and/or Compliance Committee.

Element 7:

Prompt Response to Compliance Issues

- Timely, reasonable inquiry into evidence of misconduct
- Appropriate corrective actions in response to potential violations
- Procedures to voluntarily self-report potential fraud or misconduct to funders

74237503R00124

Made in the USA
Columbia, SC
11 September 2019